TABLE OF CONTENTS

ACRONYMS

A2AD	Anti-access, Area Denial
DOD	Department of Defense
JFC	Joint Force Commander
PLA	People's Liberations Army
PRC	People's Republic of China
UN	United Nations
UNPKO	United Nations Peacekeeping Operations

ILLUSTRATIONS

iii

INTRODUCTION

The US Department of Defense (DOD) announced a shift of focus to the Asia-Pacific region in January 2012. This shift aligns with modern China's emergence as a growing economic and military power. The United States asserts that it will monitor China's growth and military modernizations and focus on increasing Chinese anti-access, area denial (A2AD) capabilities, which the United States considers a threat to regional security.[1] To counter such capabilities, the United States intends to "invest as required to ensure its ability to operate effectively" despite the presence of A2AD weapons in an operating area.[2] Chinese government documents emphasize a defensive strategic posture, yet observations of their military developments do indeed reveal a prioritization on A2AD objectives. This study seeks to gain insight on the employment of Chinese force and forces for strategic objectives as a manifestation of operational art within the People's Liberation Army (PLA).

To this end, the primary research question of this monograph asks: *Does contemporary PLA doctrine and activity indicate a uniquely Chinese way of thinking and practice in operational art, influenced by philosophy and military tradition?* The presence of a unique characterization of Chinese operational art aids US military planners supporting US Pacific Command theater engagement efforts as they seek to understand Chinese military activities. Additionally, understanding a Chinese "flavor" of operational art better informs US operational and tactical level commanders should military engagement take place.

---

[1]US Department of Defense, *Annual Report to Congress on Military and Security Developments Involving the People's Republic of China 2012* (Washington D.C.: Government Printing Office, 2012).

[2]US Department of Defense, *Sustaining US Global Leadership: Priorities for 21st Century Defense* (Washington, DC: Government Printing Office, January 2012), 5.

The underlying hypothesis rests on the premise that an ideological difference between the United States and the People's Republic of China (PRC) exists, and influences their respective use of military power. The contrasting culture, philosophy, and history of the United States and China support the likelihood of different "flavors" of operational art. These differences underpin how an individual or group perceives their place in the world, and the ways an individual or group seeks to achieve desires. Stated another way, a difference in perspective is likely to affect the ways in which means are arranged to achieve ends in all settings, including the use of military force.

This study reviews recent PLA doctrine and activities (peacekeeping, anti-piracy operations and cyber warfare), and finds they do indeed reveal a Chinese flavor of operational art. The term "flavor" conveys Chinese specifics that exist within a range of possibly universal considerations of operational art. Chinese philosophy and military tradition support noticeable differences between the PLA and Western armies, which include a higher value placed on an indirect approach, patience in decision-making and the tempo of operations, a greater emphasis on asymmetrical warfare, and the use of strategy and stratagems to attack an adversary's strategy instead of their fielded forces.

Operational Art, a Comparison of East and West Perspectives

For the purpose of this study, US Joint doctrine provides a representative source for comparison with Chinese doctrine and practice. US Joint Publication 3-0 describes operational art as:

> ...the use of creative thinking by commanders and staffs to design strategies, campaigns, and major operations and organize and employ military forces. It is a thought process that uses skill, knowledge, experience, and judgment to overcome the ambiguity and uncertainty of a complex environment and understand the problem at hand. Operational art also promotes unified action by encouraging JFCs [Joint Force Commanders] and staffs to consider the capabilities, actions, goals, priorities, and operating processes of interorganizational partners, while determining objectives, establishing priorities, and assigning tasks to subordinate forces. It facilitates the coordination, synchronization, and,

2

where appropriate, integration of military operations with those of interorganizational partners, thereby promoting unity of effort.[3]

Later, Joint Publication 3-0 summarizes operational art as the effort taken in joint operations to integrate "ends, ways, and means, while accounting for risk, across the levels of war."[4]

Contemporary Western scholars still debate when operational art first emerged. Historian Robert Epstein makes a compelling case that it first appeared in Napoleonic warfare, while Dr. James Schneider asserts that operational art emerged with the US Civil War.[5] Additionally, definitions and descriptions of operational art vary among US military service branches. This study accepts Joint Publication 3-0's description of operational art, *the creative arrangement of resources and tactical actions in major operations or campaigns, to achieve operational or strategic objectives.*[6] Within this description, the study's focus lies in identifying a uniquely Chinese practice of operational art when compared to the United States. When observed, preferences reflected in doctrine or practice of operational art reveal a flavor of operational art for a given country.

US Joint doctrine reflects a US flavor of operational art conveyed as preferences under the elements of operational design. The elements of operational design include both tools and a methodology "to conceive of and construct viable approaches to operations and campaigns."[7] Of

---

[3]Chairman, Joint Chiefs of Staff, *Joint Publication (JP) 3-0, Joint Operations* (Washington, DC: Government Printing Office, August 2011), II-3.

[4]Ibid., II-4.

[5]Robert M. Epstein, *Napoleon's Last Victory and the Emergence of Modern War* (Lawrence: University Press of Kansas, 1994), 17. James J. Schneider, *Vulcan's Anvil* (Ft Leavenworth: School of Advanced Military Studies/US Army Command and General Staff College, 1992), 1.

[6]Chairman, Joint Chiefs of Staff, *Joint Publication (JP) 3-0*, xii.

[7]Chairman, Joint Chiefs of Staff, *Joint Publication (JP) 5-0, Joint Operations Planning* (Washington, DC: Government Printing Office, August 2011), III-1.

the thirteen elements of operational design, four elements reveal a US flavor of operational art: the importance placed on termination criteria, military end-state, objectives, and direct and indirect approach. Together, termination criteria and military end-state establish conditions the United States desires and the specific role of military force in their pursuit. Termination criteria are "developed first among the elements of operational design as they enable the development of the military end state and objectives."[8] This emphasis enables US military commanders to begin planning with the end in mind, supporting a linear approach. Working back from the conceived termination criteria and military end-state, planners and commanders create objectives to focus military actions towards the defeat of the enemy's center of gravity leading to the desired military end-state.[9]

US Joint doctrine places an emphasis on pursuing a direct approach toward the desired military end-state and termination criteria. The following statement from Joint Publication 5-0, exemplifies this emphasis. Only in "the event that a direct attack is not a reasonable solution, JFCs should seek an indirect approach until conditions are established that permit successful direct attacks."[10] The commander then seeks to arrange operations, another element of operational design, by managing simultaneity, depth, timing, and tempo of operations to gain and maintain the initiative. Joint doctrine desires to "seize the initiative in all situations through decisive use of Joint force capabilities. In combat, this involves both defensive and offensive operations at the earliest possible time, forcing the enemy to culminate offensively and setting the conditions for decisive operations."[11] Taken collectively, US Joint doctrine conveys a flavor of

---

[8]Ibid., III-19.

[9]Ibid., III-20.

[10]Ibid., III-32.

[11]Joint Chiefs of Staff, Joint Publication (JP) 3-0, V-8.

4

operational art where the end is determined first and then a linear approach is established from existing conditions towards the desired end-state. The creation of objectives, as incremental steps to focus military power toward reaching the favored end-state through overwhelming combat power, further supports a US preference for a linear approach.

Francois Jullien in *A Treatise on Efficacy*, characterizes a Western perspective where individuals and groups theorize an "ideal form," a desired end state, which becomes the overriding "goal," or objective toward which all efforts are expended to "make it become fact," termination criteria and military end state.[12] Jullien describes the Western approach to action:

> With our eyes fixed on the model that we have conceived, which we project on the world and on which we base a plan to be executed, we choose to intervene in the world and give a form to reality. And the closer we stick to that ideal form in the action that we take, the better our chances of succeeding.[13]

Jullien's analysis of a larger Western perspective reinforces a characterization of a US flavor of operational art, where a desired end is "conceived," then pursued directly. The United States then seeks the initiative early and often, applying overwhelming combat power in a linear manner to the desired end state.

FOUNDATIONS OF CHINESE THINKING

The roots of a Western perspective rest deep in history and provide a contrast with Chinese thinking. Geoffrey Parker in *The Cambridge History of Warfare* writes, "Every culture develops its own way of war" and includes a reference from Sun Tzu where, "To subdue the enemy without fighting is the acme of skill." He then contrasts this Chinese approach to warfare,

---

[12]Francois Jullien, *A Treatise on Efficacy* (Hawaii, Honolulu: University of Hawaii Press, 2004), 1.

[13]Ibid.

in the remainder of the book, with a Western way of warfare characterized by technological

solutions, emphasis on training and discipline, a focus on destroying the enemy, a "challenge and

response dynamic," and the ability to finance all of these.[14] Support for a uniquely Chinese flavor

of operational art resides in the difference between Eastern and Western philosophy and military

traditions. The West rests largely on a Judeo-Christian worldview with Carl von Clausewitz best

representing its military tradition. China rests on the philosophical influence of Confucius,

Taoism, and the military tradition marked by Sun Tzu, among other ancient military writings.

Chinese scholar Andrew Scobell claims the argument for a unique Chinese approach to military

strategy is a commonly held view by "both Chinese and non-Chinese soldiers, scholars, and

analysts."[15] He acknowledges the existence of "key commonalities across strategic traditions"

while maintaining, "there are important and distinctive cultural elements within traditions."[16] This

study seeks reflections of distinctive cultural elements that highlight US and Chinese flavors

within the universal aspects of operational art.

Patrick Porter's *Military Orientalism: Eastern War through Western Eyes* provides a

caution against viewing manifestations of Eastern warfare as inherently different. Instead of

viewing culture as determining behavior, Porter defines culture as "an ambiguous repertoire of

competing ideas that can be selected, instrumentalised, and manipulated, instead of a clear script

---

[14]*The Cambridge History of Warfare*, edited by Geoffrey Parker. (New York: Cambridge University Press, 2005), 2. Parker includes the following as Western principals of war: "reliance on superior technology," discipline and training, continuity within the Western military tradition - including a focus on the destruction of the enemy, a "challenge and response dynamic," and lastly the ability to economically support such efforts to adapt and change.

[15]Andrew Scobell, "The Chinese Way of War," in *The Evolution of Operational Art from Napoleon to the Present*, edited by John Andreas Olsen and Martin Van Creveld, 195-221 (New York: Oxford University Press Inc., 2011), 195.

[16]Ibid.

6

for action."[17] He supports his claim by weighting "the impact of external stimuli and the dynamic action/reaction reciprocity of war," examining apparent "contradictions within cultures, the multiplicity of strategic cultures in one country or society, and the way it is politically usable."[18] Finally, Porter cautions against a simplification of cultural differences, stating that a view of "culture should be attentive to the crossovers and interconnectedness of war, so that culture is not reducible to a discourse of difference and separation."[19] Warfare further highlights the risk of over simplification because each opposing side is drawn to "imitation and interpenetration" with their opponent, and evolves throughout a conflict.[20] While not specifically addressing the Chinese, Porter's thesis identifies risks in labeling philosophical or cultural differences as specific determining factors that characterize how a nation approaches the conduct of war. When taken together, the existing literature accepts that cultural influences are likely to be more distinct at a strategic level, while their impact is likely less visible at lower levels of war where pragmatism takes precedence due to the pending immediacy of results.

The realm of operational art bridges the strategic and tactical levels of war. As a result, a focus on operational art increases the likelihood of observing cultural flavors in military operations. Porter's view lessens the deterministic view of philosophy or culture and accepts that countries in opposition are likely to adjust and weigh different aspects of their respective culture based on pragmatic rationale, while retaining a link to their historic foundations. The following

[17]Patrick Porter, *Military Orientalism: Eastern War through Western Eyes* (New York: Columbia University Press, 2009), 15.

[18]Ibid., 16.

[19]Ibid., 194.

[20]Ibid., 195

7

section introduces the foundational pillars of Chinese philosophy and related concepts in China's military tradition.

Chinese Philosophy & Military Tradition

Huston Smith in *The World's Religions*, comments on the influence of Confucius on Chinese culture, writing that the Chinese "reverently speak of him as the first teacher - not that there were no teachers before him, but because he stands first in rank."[21] Smith asserts that the teachings of Confucius serve as a "deliberate tradition" created as a "prototype of what the Chinese hoped the Chinese Character would become."[22] Regarding the degree to which Confucianism remains prevalent within China, many government positions require knowledge of Confucian writings.[23]

Confucianism in contemporary China likely continues to reinforce social control and management of the population.[24] Central to Confucian belief is one's identity or notion of self. The Confucian philosophy places an individual's identity at the "center of relationships" where the notion of self is based on one's relationships with other people, and is "defined by the sum of its social roles."[25] The resulting construct encourages individuals to seek harmony within all relationships. Roger Ames expounds on this idea: "the exemplary person pursues harmony (*ho*),

---

[21]Houston Smith, *The World's Religions* (New York: Harper Collins Publishers, 1991), 154.

[22]Houston Smith, *The World's Religions, Revised and Updated* (New York: Harper Collins, Inc.. Kindle Edition, 2009), Kindle Location 3594.

[23]Ibid., Kindle Locations 3337-3338.

[24]Ibid., Kindle Locations 3948, 3953-3954.

[25]Ibid., Kindle Locations 3785-3786.

not sameness," where the individual attempts to "make the most of any situation."[26] Always

striving for harmony in the "quality of the combination at any one moment created by effectively

correlating and contextualizing" all available means.[27] Ames contrasts this with the Western view

that a person is a "discrete individual defined in terms of some inherent nature" which stems from

ancient Greek and Judeo-Christian beliefs.[28] This contrasting viewpoint has the Western

individual believing they are separate and discreet from others and the environment in which they

act, while the Chinese individual seeks harmony within their environment and in relations with

others. The difference in perspective affects how one seeks a desired change. The Western

individual attempts to compel surroundings into a desired state, while the Chinese attempts to

exist within the environment in a state of harmony to bring about change. The influence of

harmony does not imply a lack of desire for change or not pursuing change. Instead, concepts

within the Taoist philosophy reveal how a Chinese individual can seek desired conditions while

maintaining harmony.

Taoism, as revealed in the *Tao Te Ching*, meaning "The Way and Its Power," traces back

to the sixth century B.C.[29] *Tao*, translated "path" or "way" is concerned with how the practitioner

can leverage the power, *te*, within the Tao. A key aspect in the pursuit of the *te*, is the notion of

wu wei, which "translates literally as inaction" however in Taoism implies "pure effectiveness

and creative quietude" with the reduction of friction in action.[30]

---

[26]*Sun-Tzu The Art of Warfare*, trans. and ed. Roger T. Ames (New York: Ballantine Books, 1993), 59.

[27]Ibid., 59, 62.

[28]Ibid., 58, 59.

[29]Smith, *The World's Religions,* Kindle Locations 4123, 4136.

[30]Ibid., Kindle Locations 4190-4191, 4337.

Wu wei is illustrated by water, "infinitely supple, yet incomparably strong."[31] *Wu wei* requires that an individual seek solitude while attempting to resist both the immediate stimuli taking place around them, and their passions. Only in solitude, reached through deliberate patience, can the practitioner reach a state where they are able to observe the intricacies of a given situation. This in turn leads to a greater overall understanding from which actions and decisions are better informed.[32] The resulting decisions and actions should flow "spontaneously," like "water adapts itself to its surroundings and seeks out the lowest places," or "the empty spaces in life and nature."[33] Smith characterizes the individual who manages the concept of *wu wei* as one who "acts without strain, persuades without argument, is eloquent without flourish, and achieves results without violence, coercion, or pressure. Though the agent may be scarcely noticed, his or her influence is in fact decisive."[34] A quote from Sun Tzu illustrates this concept, "To subdue the enemy without fighting is the acme of skill."[35]

By applying *wu wei*, one can adjust their position within a given environment, save energy, and reduce risks or opposition. The result is acting in a manner where others begin to "do the pushing for you," propelling you forward.[36] The good practitioner of *wu wei* experiences lasting conditions as the change in relative position is viewed as part of an emerging reality versus having been achieved through the direct application of force to impose one's will on

---

[31]Ibid., Kindle Locations 4398-4399.

[32]Ibid., Kindle Locations 4409-4411.

[33]Ibid., Kindle Locations 4348, 4382, 4366-4367.

[34]Ibid., Kindle Locations 4400-4401.

[35]*Sun-Tzu The Art of Warfare*, trans. and ed. Roger T. Ames, 111.

[36]Jullien, *A Treatise on Efficacy on Efficacy*, 115.

another, creating strife and competition.[37] Others are likely to accept the resulting change more positively.

Ames' commentary in Sun-Tzu *The Art of Warfare*, links the philosophical influences of Confucianism and Taoism, with the related subjects of warfare and wisdom in early Chinese texts. Ames highlights the philosophical impacts of harmony, where an individual views their "specific place in the world" as within a "continuous, uninterrupted process."[38] This contrasts with the Western view where individuals exist with a definite start and end.[39] Additionally, the Chinese view of existing within a continuous process highlights the Taoist idea of *yin* and *yang*. Instead of viewing opposites as unrelated, this classic Chinese perspective accepts "change in the quality of relationships between things ... on a continuum as movement between such polar oppositions."[40] Smith characterizes *yin* and *yang* where *yin* reflects one polarity of opposites that include good, active, positive, light, summer, and male. In contrast, *yang* represents the opposite, and includes evil, passive, negative, dark, winter, and female. Depicted, *yin* and *yang* exist together "circling around each other" and "represent the two indigenous poles of the Chinese character."[41] Ralph Sawyer in Sun Tzu *Art of War* provides an example where Sun Tzu used "some forty paired, mutually interrelated categories" to analyze a situation.[42] Analysis revealing an enemy advantage in any set of *yin* and *yang*-related pairs leads the commander to take actions

---

[37]Jullien, *A Treatise on Efficacy*, 115.

[38]*Sun-Tzu The Art of Warfare*, trans. and ed. Roger T. Ames, 50.

[39]Ibid., 50.

[40]*Sun-Tzu The Art of Warfare*, trans. and ed. Roger T. Ames, 76. Smith, *The World's Religions*, Kindle Locations 4493-4494.

[41]Smith, *The World's Religions*, Kindle Locations 4567-4569.

[42]*Sun Tzu, Art of War*, trans. and ed. Ralph D. Sawyer (Colorado: Westview Press, 1994), 130-131.

to "convert the enemy's superiority into weakness."[43] This concept recognizes the "interdependence and correlative character" of polar opposites, which are "explained by reference to each other," and implies the ability to alter a situation into its polar opposite, where the weak can act in a given situation to become the strong.[44]

The key philosophical concepts of *ho* (harmony), *wu wei* (illustrated by water as purely effective, supple, strong, and adaptive), and *yin* and *yang* (perspective of continuous cycle between opposite, yet interrelated, polarities) are uniquely Chinese. Ames asserts that Chinese philosophy "resists severe distinction between theory and application" where the philosophy is acted out in practice.[45] This claim underpins a Chinese approach to all aspects of life, which by extension includes an approach to or flavor of operational art. Sun Tzu's *The Art of War* builds on the philosophical ideas discussed above and reflects the Chinese military tradition.

Chinese scholar David Lai describes the Chinese concept of *shi* in Sun Tzu's *The Art of War* as part of "a strategy China uses to exploit the 'strategic configuration of power' to its advantage and maximize its ability to preserve its national independence and develop its comprehensive national power."[46] As Sun Tzu states, "those skilled at making the enemy move

---

[43]Ibid., 131.

[44]*Sun-Tzu The Art of Warfare*, trans. and ed. Roger T. Ames, 52, 78.

[45]Ibid., 41.

[46]David Lai, *Learning from the Stones: A GO Approach to Mastering China's Strategic Concept, Shi* (Carlisle, PA: Strategic Studies Institute, 2004), 2. Lai presents four unique implications that exist within the concept of shi. First, it includes both the "zheng" or "regular way of doing things" and the "extraordinary (qi) ways" of combining actions. Second, shi includes a concern with "creating an overwhelming force with irresistible unleashing power." The third concept of shi includes "developing a favorable situation with great potential to achieve the political objective." Lastly, the fourth aspect of shi is "about taking and maintaining the initiative."

do so by creating a situation to which he must conform."[47] Jullien includes *Shi* as one of two aspects of Chinese strategy, describing it as "the notion of potential" that exists within the "situation or configuration (*xing*) as it develops and takes shape before your eyes (as a relation of forces)," and can be manipulated to a position of advantage.[48] Jullien quotes Sun Tzu to illustrate such potential: "In combat, troops are used by the victor like accumulated water for which one opens up a breach in the precipice."[49] The similarity to *wu wei* is evident, creating an expectation of Chinese troops positioned in a location of potential, then employed like water flowing from high to low, to "avoid the points at which the enemy is strong and attack it where it is weak," where the "enemy is 'empty' – deficient or unprepared."[50] Jullien captures the difference between Western and Chinese thinking (emphasis in original):

> [T]he difference between Western and Chinese thought: one [the West] *constructs* a model that is then projected onto the situation, which implies that the situation is momentarily 'frozen.' The other [the Chinese] relies on the situation as on a disposition that is known to be constantly evolving. It is a disposition that functions as a device …a particular configuration that can be manipulated and that *in itself* produces an effect.[51]

The potential (*shi*) is a result of specific conditions within a situation, including the environment, the nature of the enemy and one's own forces. By conforming to the situation (*wu wei*), water flows to an "irresistible and irreversible" point (*shi*) from which it is released and victory grasped.[52]

---

[47]Lai, *Learning from the Stones*, 2.

[48]Jullien, *A Treatise on Efficacy*, 17.

[49]Ibid., 172.

[50]Ibid., 172-173.

[51]Ibid., 189-190

[52]Ibid., 176-177.

Lai, in his study contrasting the popular Chinese game of "Go" to American games (chess, poker, boxing, and American football), illustrates that a "clear difference exists between the Chinese and American (Western) ways of war and diplomacy."[53] He asserts the Chinese "place heavy emphasis on strategy and stratagems whereas the West relies more on overwhelming force and advanced capability."[54] To support his claim, Lai quotes Russell F. Weigley regarding an American way of war, which "uses massive power, excels in advanced technology, and pursues total victory." [55] In contrast, the Chinese emphasize "deception," a desire to "attack the enemy's strategy," to "win through unexpected moves," the use of "the soft and gentle to overcome the hard and strong," and to "stay clear of the enemy's main force and strike at his weak point."[56] Lai concludes the "Chinese way of war and diplomacy is in striking difference to the Western way of war" where the Chinese stress strategy and stratagems to determine "how one can win from the position of the weak."[57]

Jullien's treatise provides insightful contrasts in comparing Clausewitz's *On War* with Sun Tzu's *Art of War* to illustrate differences between Western and Chinese military traditions. The fundamental difference lies in the lens through which each views the interworking of the world at large. Jullien asserts the Western approach includes a view of "efficacy on the basis of abstract, ideal forms, set up as models to be projected onto to the world and that our [Western] will deliberately establishes as a goal to be attained."[58] In contrast, the Chinese approach includes

---

[53]Lai, *Learning from the Stones*, 30.

[54]Ibid., 3.

[55]Ibid., 4,5.

[56]Ibid.

[57]Ibid., 5, 31.

[58]Jullien, *A Treatise on Efficacy*, vii.

a "concept of efficacy that teaches one to learn how to allow an effect to come about: not to aim for it (directly) but to implicate it (as a consequence), in other words not to seek it, but simply to welcome it – to allow it to result."[59] Sun Tzu provides a useful comparison, which emphasizes both detailed analysis of the situation and an indirect approach. Sun Tzu, in his chapter on military disposition states, "the victorious army first realizes the conditions for victory, and then seeks to engage in battle. The vanquished army fights first, and then seeks victory."[60] Culturally, the Chinese appear less inclined to begin with the end in mind as proposed in US doctrine, instead they "consider the potential of a situation to be variable; it cannot be determined in advance, since it proceeds from continuous adaptation."[61]

Regarding initiative in military action, Chinese military writings provide a layered perspective. Jullien describes the Chinese perspective as patient, allowing initiative to emerge, specifically that "initiative is revealed not at the beginning but rather at the end, for it too stems from an ongoing development, is acquired little by little and is manifested in the form of a result."[62] Additionally, Lai describes one aspect of the meaning of *shi* (of the four implied), as efforts to take and maintain the initiative. Again, "As Sun Tzu puts it, 'those skilled at making the enemy move do so by creating a situation to which he must conform.'"[63] This layered approach to initiative supports an indirect approach, taking actions that allow the initiative to emerge then using initiative to further act within the situation to maintain the initiative. This differs from US Joint doctrine which stresses the desire to "seize the initiative in all situations" through the use of

---

[59]Jullien, *A Treatise on Efficacy*, vii.

[60]*Sun Tzu, Art of War*, trans. and ed. Ralph D. Sawyer, 184.

[61]Jullien, *A Treatise on Efficacy*, 23.

[62]Ibid., 163-164.

[63]Lai, *Learning from the Stones*, 2.

"defensive and offensive operations at the earliest possible time, forcing the enemy to culminate offensively and setting the conditions for decisive operations," clearly reflecting the high value placed on speed and tempo and an overall direct approach.[64]

To summarize the resulting difference in respective military traditions, the West favors a direct approach to reaching a preconceived end state while the Chinese appear to favor an indirect approach based on critical analysis the situation, self, and the enemy. Once determined, the Chinese attempt to manage a situation through patience, surprise, and asymmetry, to undermine the strengths of the enemy while taking advantage of emerging opportunities. Additionally, the existence of a uniquely Chinese philosophy and military tradition is reflected in the combination of seeming opposites (*yin* and *yang*), flexible applications of forces (*wu wei*), and taken comprehensively, the use of operations to create potential, or, a position of advantage (*shi*), as the situation develops.

CHINESE DOCTRINE

The following exploration seeks to identify the degree to which Chinese documents reflect both the existence of operational art and the presence of unique philosophical and historical underpinnings. Examined documents include "China's National Defense," released by the Information Office of the State Council of the PRC, which provides a national perspective on Chinese strategy and PLA references. *Unrestricted Warfare* and *The Science of Military Strategy*, both published by the PLA, provide insight into PLA doctrine. The use of Chinese-language source materials introduces risks in translation of content and the nature of the publication in general. Chinese scholar Andrew Scobell highlights a concern that Chinese government-released publications "may express empty, high minded rhetoric to mask unprincipled motives and justify

---

[64]Joint Chiefs of Staff, *Joint Publication (JP) 3-0*, V-8.

16

erratic behaviors."[65] The use of United States Government documents as secondary sources

mitigate this risk within this study. This examination reveals a Chinese flavor of operational art

supported by the doctrinal principles of a holistic approach, tailored combinations of resources

and means, and the importance of information. These doctrinal principles are supported by the

philosophical concepts of harmony, yin yang, and *wu wei*, and reflect China's military tradition of

an indirect approach, stratagems, and asymmetry.

China's National Defense

The Information Office of the State Council of the PRC releases "China's National

Defense" policy approximately every two years. These documents, often referred to as *The White*

Papers, communicate China's official view on national defense in the context of their respective

security situation, serving a function similar to the US National Security Strategy. The majority of

content focuses on aspects of internal defense, functions of the PLA in support of the Chinese

Communist Party and internal stability of the population. *The White Papers* also address external

activities concerning China's defense in general and PLA activities in particular. According to the

2012 US Department of Defense (DOD) annual report to Congress concerning China, the

strategic objectives of China have been largely unchanged over the last ten years and include:

"preserving Communist Party rule, sustaining economic growth and development, defending

national sovereignty and territorial integrity, achieving national unification, maintaining internal

stability, and securing China's status as a great power."[66]

---

[65]Andrew Scobell, *China's Use of Military Force, Beyond the Great Wall and the Long March* (New York: Cambridge University Press, 2003). 8.

[66]Department of Defense, *Military and Security Developments Involving the People's Republic of China 2012* (Washington D.C.: Office of the Secretary of Defense, May 2012), 2.

The White Papers characterize the essence of operational art in describing the PLA as one element integrated within a whole of government approach, where the PLA is a supporting force to other elements of national power. Specifically, under the current Chinese strategy of "Active Defense," the PLA seeks "close coordination between military struggle and political, economic, diplomatic, cultural, and legal endeavors, uses strategies and tactics in a comprehensive way, and takes the initiative to prevent and defuse crises and deter conflicts and wars."[67] This use of strategies and tactics in a comprehensive manner reflects the concept of harmony, pursuit of the "quality of the combination at any one moment created by effectively correlating and contextualizing" all available means into a holistic mass with synergistic potential, or *shi*.[68]

Central to all *White Papers* released since 1998 is China's claim that its security policies are defensive in nature and that China desires peace (*harmony*) in and beyond the Pacific region. The 2010 *White Papers* clearly assert, "China unswervingly takes the road of peaceful development, strives to build a harmonious socialist society internally, and promotes the building of a harmonious world enjoying lasting peace and common prosperity externally."[69] The resulting strategy, termed "Active Defense," provides overarching guidance for the PLA. China claims a strategic defensive posture allows them to "attack only after being attacked."[70] Active Defense

---

[67]The People's Republic of China, *China's National Defense in 2008* (Beijing: Information Office of the State Council of the People's Republic of China, 2009).

[68]*Sun-Tzu The Art of Warfare*, trans. and ed. Roger T. Ames, 59, 62.

[69]The People's Republic of China, *China's National Defense in 2010* (Beijing: Information Office of the State Council of the People's Republic of China, 2011).

[70]Department of Defense, *Military and Security Developments Involving the People's Republic of China 2012* (Washington D.C.: Office of the Secretary of Defense, May 2012), 3, 25. On Page 25, DOD reporting highlights the uncertainty that exists surrounding what China considers an attack that would trigger its response. The range of possible triggers may include "political action" resulting in a situation where "PLA forces might be employed preemptively in the nature of defense."

rests on maintaining a strategic defensive posture from which offensive operations can take place, and stresses the introduction of advanced technologies and information superiority as vital in modern warfare.

As early as 2002, *The White Papers* show China openly identifying information assets as key to winning contemporary wars. This emphasis increased in scope and clarity in 2004, which conveyed the long-term aim of PLA modernization in terms of information. Specifically, the "PLA, aiming at building an informationalized force and winning an informationalized war, deepens its reform, dedicates itself to innovation, improves its quality and actively pushes forward the RMA [revolution in military affairs] with Chinese characteristics with informationalization at the core."[71] The 2012 US DOD report to Congress, *Military and Security Developments Involving the People's Republic of China*, characterized the PLA's desire to win "local wars under conditions of informatization" as resting on the use of "advanced computer systems, information technology, and communications networks to gain operational advantage over an opponent."[72] The DOD report asserts that China's growing emphasis on information is an "essential element, if not a fundamental prerequisite, of China's emerging anti-access/area-denial regime in the ability to control and dominate the information spectrum in all dimensions of the modern battlespace."[73] *The White Papers* support this claim by revealing Chinese efforts in modernization, training, research, and integrated joint exercises at the operational level. These

---

[71]The People's Republic of China, *China's National Defense in 2004* (Beijing: Information Office of the State Council of the People's Republic of China, 2004). For more information on revolutions in military affairs, see MacGregor Knox and Williamson Murray, eds., *The Dynamics of Military Revolution, 1300-2050* (Cambridge, UK.: Cambridge University Press, 2001).

[72]Department of Defense, *Military and Security Developments Involving the People's Republic of China 2012*, 3.

[73]Department of Defense, *Military and Security Developments Involving the People's Republic of China 2010* (Washington D.C.: Office of the Secretary of Defense, 2010), 30.

efforts seek to better prepare commanders in conjunction with the guidance contained in Active

Defense doctrine, and networked systems to command and control integrated joint operations.[74]

The 2008 *White Paper* describing Chinese guidelines for winning local wars under

conditions of informationization reveals the continued influence of *shi*, *wu wei*, *yin* and *yang*,

stratagems, and asymmetry (emphasis added):

> Meeting the requirements of confrontation between war systems in modern warfare and taking integrated joint operations as the basic approach, it is designed to bring the operational strengths of different services and arms into full play, *combine offensive operations with defensive operations*, give priority to the *flexible application* of strategies and tactics, *seek advantages and avoid disadvantages*, and make the best use of our *strong points to attack the enemy's weak points*. It endeavors to refine the command system for joint operations, the joint training system and the joint support system, optimize the structure and composition of forces, and speed up the building of a combat force structure suitable for winning local wars in conditions of informationization.[75]

An examination of "China's National Defense" policy provides insight into further aspects of a

Chinese flavor of operation art with emphasis on technology and information. At first reading, the

stress placed on technology and informatization appears very similar to Parker's inclusion of

technology as a characteristic of Western war. However, upon further analysis the Chinese focus

on technology and information appears to have two purposes. First, it is aimed at negating enemy

strengths and second, as a control mechanism in warfare. PLA technology and information appear

in line with developing stratagems and asymmetric advantages in contrast to Western reliance on

technology for a direct defeat of an enemy. Additionally, the philosophical concepts of harmony,

yin and *yang*, and *wu wei* remain identifiable characteristics within the publications of "China's

National Defense." PLA doctrine further elaborates an underlying emphasis on these concepts.

---

[74]The People's Republic of China, *China's National Defense in 2004*.

[75]The People's Republic of China, *China's National Defense in 2008* (Beijing: Information Office of the State Council of the People's Republic of China, 2009).

<u>The People's Liberation Army's Doctrine</u>

This study uses two primary sources, *Unrestricted Warfare*, and *The Science of Military Strategy* to examine PLA doctrine for operational art. *Unrestricted Warfare*, written in 1999 by two PLA colonels, conveys PLA doctrinal changes made after the 1991 Gulf War. David Lai asserts the influence of Sun Tzu on Qiao Liang and Wang Xiangsui, stressing the similarity of Sun Tzu's *Art of War* where the weak can overpower the strong using "unconventional approaches."[76] *The Science of Military Strategy* was released in Chinese in 2001 and later translated into English. Both sources were published under PLA institutions, the PLA Literature and Arts Publishing House, and the PLA Academy of Military Science, respectfully. Publication under PLA auspices indicates a degree of professional acceptance of their content. Together these works provide PLA doctrine for examination.

Chinese observations of US and coalition operations in the 1991 Gulf War acted as the catalyst to drive an emphasis on technology and information within the PLA. The authors of *Unrestricted Warfare,* Qiao Liang and Wang Xiangsui, highlight the Gulf War as an emerging age in warfare, dubbed "unrestricted warfare," where "all boundaries lying between the two worlds of war and non-war, of military and non-military, will be totally destroyed."[77] After the Gulf War, PLA doctrine reveals three areas for increased emphasis: first, an emphasis on a holistic approach to war with the PLA as one element among many elements of Chinese national power; second, an emphasis on creative approaches to the employment of resources in conventional and nonconventional ways; and lastly, the importance of information in warfare.

---

[76]David Lai, *Learning from the Stones*, 31.

[77]Qiao Liang and Wang Xiangsui, *Unrestricted Warfare, China's Master Plan to Destroy America* (Panama City, Panama: Pan American Publishing Company, 2002), 5.

In line with "China's National Defense," *Unrestricted Warfare*, and *The Science of Military Strategy* reflect the desire and need for a holistic approach to national security, utilizing the entirety of national resources. *The Science of Military Strategy* addresses both military and non-military assets in warfare where economic instruments of power are the "foundation," political instruments are the "denominator," and military capabilities serve as the "backup force."[78] Multidimensional coordination, a PLA principle of warfare, illustrates this holistic approach by stressing that military and nonmilitary entities should work in concert towards common objectives. Multidimensional coordination occurs at and between all levels of war, includes strategic resources and instruments of power and efforts to leverage international organizations to shape the environment.[79]

PLA doctrine includes the term "campaigning-operational art" as a level of war. Translated, "campaigning" implies either the "war arts or art of warfare," stressing creativity.[80] Creative artistry is further evident in PLA efforts to act holistically. PLA doctrine encourages the commander to creatively combine military and nonmilitary resources in both conventional and nonconventional ways, revealing insight into a Chinese flavor of operational art. In order to manage possibilities within a holistic approach, Qiao and Wang stress the desire to "find the optimum way to achieve objectives, a correct and effective way to employ means. In other words, to find out how to combine different means and create new means to achieve objectives."[81]

---

[78]Peng Quangqian and Yao Youzhi, *The Science of Military Strategy* (Military Science Publishing House, Academy of Military Science of the Chinese People's Liberations Army, 2005), 210.

[79]Qiao Liang and Wang Xiangsui, *Unrestricted Warfare*, 183-184.

[80]Ibid., 170.

[81]Ibid., 167.

PLA doctrine uses the terms "combining" and "additive" to stress creativity in task organizing capabilities. The desire of combinations is to best integrate existing and emerging technologies and conventional and unconventional tactics within a given situation. Qiao and Wang describe a gifted Chinese military leader in the ability to break from existing paradigms to succeed in "consciously combining all of the means available at the time to play the ageless masterpiece by changing the tonality of the war."[82] Seeking combinations exposes a contemporary term demonstrating the continuing influence of *ho,* or harmony. As described by Ames, the individual strives for harmony in the "quality of the combination at any one moment created by effectively correlating and contextualizing" all available means.[83] In this manner, the Chinese stress a creative fusion of holistic means by "combining the battlefield and non-battlefield, warfare and non-warfare, military and non-military."[84]

The Chinese have dubbed the phrase "modified combined war that goes beyond limits" to stress the multitude of possible combinations in the pursuit of victory.[85] Considerations include: international organizations, activities, entities and organizations located outside the immediate area of operations make no distinction between military and non-military and surpass all levels of war to include tactical actions. When all means are considered holistically, a combination tailored to a situation is selected. The result implies the creation of a "composite force in all aspects related to national interests" with the ability to serve traditional military functions and non-

---

[82]Ibid., 118.

[83]*Sun-Tzu The Art of Warfare*, trans. and ed. Roger T. Ames, 59, 62.

[84]Qiao Liang and Wang Xiangsui, *Unrestricted Warfare*, 120.

[85]Ibid., 155.

23

military functions in achieving national goals.[86] When employed, the success of the force can "become severe and begin to be shocking," releasing their *shi* on the adversary.[87]

A second aspect of creative artistry in PLA doctrine builds on the philosophical concept of *yin* and *yang*. The Chinese do not view superiority as an all-encompassing static end state. Instead, the Chinese view superiority as variable across the realm of warfare and over time. The concept of *yin* and *yang* illustrates the PLA point of view that relative strength and weakness exist as poles on a continuum. Chinese doctrine reflects the ability to alter one's position in relative strength through the creative employment of combinations guided by the principle of asymmetry. The Chinese describe asymmetry as maximizing one's primary force where unexpected by the enemy. PLA doctrine stresses that asymmetry applies from initial "force disposition and employment," from planning an attack to the end of an operation.[88] Used in this manner, a tailored combination uses its relative strength in an asymmetric manner to change relative strength towards victory. Applied correctly, "the soft and gentle" can overpower the "hard and strong" or victory can be gained over the "high-tech with low-tech."[89]

The third PLA area of emphasis is a need to control and wield information based on its role in US military success. The Chinese viewed information as important in shaping popular support and understanding of a conflict through media coverage. Additionally, information helped speed decision timelines through rapid data transmission between intelligence sensors and among weapons systems. Qiao and Wang reveal Chinese emphasis on information in modern warfare, to the extent they assert that military force is not likely sufficient for victory without

---

[86]Ibid., 97-98.

[87]Ibid., 120.

[88]Ibid., 181-182.

[89]Peng Quangqian and Yao Youzhi, *The Science of Military Strategy*, 430-432.

24

integrated information superiority.[90] *The Science of Military Strategy* also highlights information as the key node linking weapons, systems, command and control devices, and individuals. This view of information underpins Chinese efforts to modernize the technology level of the PLA.

Another aspect of information adopted within Chinese doctrine is an emphasis on information operations as a force multiplier, where few skilled operators integrated across the PLA can have large relative impacts on an adversary.[91] PLA doctrine reveals two pillars of information operations, both applicable to this study: first what the Chinese deem "intelligence warfare"; and second, "cyber warfare." The Chinese include intelligence warfare under information operations. Chinese intelligence warfare includes efforts to gain access to an enemy's intelligence while protecting one's own. China conducts "cyber-intelligence warfare" to target the "cyberized battlefield" or information residing on computers or computer networks. The methods used to acquire information include traditional intelligence collection and cyber based techniques.[92]

The second pillar of information operations is cyber warfare proper. Chinese cyber warfare includes "all kinds of operational actions taken in cyber space" with the intent to "disintegrate, damage, or destroy key computers and computer networks as well as the information stored in them."[93] Overall, the PLA considers cyber activities "as both a key enabler of modern warfare and a critical new spectrum of conflict in its own right" with both offensive and defensive roles.[94] Throughout the remainder of this study, use of the term "cyber activity"

---

[90]Qiao Liang and Wang Xiangsui, *Unrestricted Warfare,* 61.

[91]Peng Quangqian and Yao Youzhi, eds., *The Science of Military Strategy*, 336-341.

[92]Ibid., 341.

[93]Ibid., 343.

[94]US-China Economic and Security Review Commission, *2009 Report to Congress,*

implies both efforts to collect intelligence through intelligence warfare and the ability to conduct cyber warfare proper.

The three areas developed after the 1991 Gulf war (a holistic approach, creativity in tailored combinations, and the importance of information) provide a snapshot of expected emphasis in Chinese strategy and PLA operations. Information acts as a both a central node and enabler. As a central node, information enables Chinese commanders to gain understanding in a given situation for creative decisions regarding combinations. The resources used in any given combination are likely to include extra-PLA forces or resources that reside within other elements of national power. Even in a limited engagement, Chinese doctrine suggests multiple elements of Chinese national power will attempt to shape a situation to an advantage. The next section examines PLA principles of war related to a Chinese flavor of operational art.

The 2012 DOD report to Congress presents Chinese "Military Strategic Guidelines" for the PLA. As conveyed, the concept of "active defense" is the overarching guidance for all PLA branches "on how to fight and win wars."[95] Active defense includes warfighting principles that emphasize the use of "precise and well timed offensive operations, gaining and retaining the initiative, attacking only under favorable conditions and exploiting an opponent's most vulnerable weaknesses."[96]

Chinese doctrine reflected in *Unrestricted Warfare* recognizes eight principles when preparing for war. These include limited objectives, unlimited measures, asymmetry, multidimensional coordination, omnidirectionality, synchrony, minimal consumption, and

---

111th Congress, 1st session (Washington D.C.: Government Printing Office, 2009). 171.

[95]Department of Defense, *Military and Security Developments Involving the People's Republic of China 2012*, 3.

[96]Ibid.

adjustment and control of the entire process.[97] The reading of PLA doctrine presents a challenge inherent in translated documents; translation introduces a loss in fidelity where the translated text may lack contextual and or implied understanding. The principles that follow appear unique and different. However, upon closer examination significant similarities exist with US military doctrinal concepts. Where similarities exist, US military doctrinal concepts are included. Qiao and Wang stress the cumulative effect of these principles when applied in practice. If followed, these principles enable Chinese commanders to face uncertainties regardless of location or a specific enemy.[98] The first four -- limited objectives, unlimited measures, asymmetry, and multidimensional coordination -- uncover contemporary displays of philosophical concepts and China's military tradition.

The first two principles (limited objectives and unlimited measures) are related. The Chinese stress limited objectives in operations to increase the likelihood of success. Limited objectives result in an advantageous force ratio and manage tempo to ensure combat power is available for subsequent operations. Limited objectives are identified after careful planning and analysis of all variables associated with an operation and victory. If analysis reveals that victory is not likely, "one must be cautions and await the [right] opportunity."[99] This emphasizes patience in waiting for "favorable conditions" in the situation to develop before acting.[100] Once analysis is complete and a plan established, the plan serves as a guide, not a regimented playbook of sequenced actions. PLA doctrine encourages flexibility throughout mission execution to support

---

[97]Qiao Liang and Wang Xiangsui, *Unrestricted Warfare,* 177.

[98]Ibid., 185.

[99]Peng Quangqian and Yao Youzhi, eds., *The Science of Military Strategy*, 239.

[100]Department of Defense, *Military and Security Developments Involving the People's Republic of China 2012*, 3.

initiative at multiple echelons to seize opportunities. The Chinese even stress understanding before acting flexible during mission execution. Commanders should balance "bravery with patience and boldness, with caution."[101] Lastly, objectives should assess the likelihood of success, be conveyed in "time and space" and allow for subsequent operations. Adhering to limited objectives help PLA operations avoid the "disastrous consequences" of failure when seeking objectives that exceed resources.[102] Limited objectives stress patience in waiting for a favorable situation before acting with a favorable force ratio towards a given objective, in order to reduce risk, and posture the force for subsequent limited objectives.[103]

The related concept of unlimited measures empowers a commander to seek all possible resources available, then apply them without "restrictions, beyond boundaries, to accomplish limited objectives."[104] The result is a creative combination, a tailored composite force that surpasses common or existing tactics, techniques, or procedures applied against a limited objective further increasing the likelihood of success.[105] Qiao and Wang illustrate this concept where "a smart general does not make his measures limited because his objectives are limited. This would very likely lead to failure on the verge of success."[106] Taken together, limited objectives and unlimited resources emphasize creating the right force to be employed at the right time in a given situation. Together these principles reflect the patience and flexibility associated

---

[101]Peng Quangqian and Yao Youzhi, eds., *The Science of Military Strategy*, 240-241.

[102]Qiao Liang and Wang Xiangsui, *Unrestricted Warfare*, 179-180.

[103]Qiao Liang and Wang Xiangsui, *Unrestricted Warfare*, 179. Peng Quangqian and Yao Youzhi, *The Science of Military Strategy*, 239.

[104]Qiao Liang and Wang Xiangsui, *Unrestricted Warfare*, 181.

[105]Ibid., 180-181.

[106]Ibid., 181.

with *wu wei* in allowing a situation to develop, *shi* in building a power potential of unlimited measures until they can be released in asymmetrically favorable conditions to successfully obtain a limited objective.

Contemporary Chinese doctrine continues a focus on seeking an asymmetric advantage in warfare. Sun Tzu wrote "just as the flow of water avoid the high grounds and rushes to the lowest point, so on the path to victory avoid the enemy's strong points and strike where he is weak."[107] As previously covered, asymmetry remains a principle of war and seeks to attack an enemy's weaknesses with one's strengths. A link exists between the principle of asymmetric warfare and the military tradition emphasizing stratagems. Chinese analyst and scholar Timothy Thomas quotes Taiwanese author Chen Wei-K'uan's description of stratagems in steps taken to "force an enemy to make a mistake which can then be taken advantage of."[108] Asymmetric warfare seeks to undermine stronger adversaries through attacks on their weakest point or leveraging stratagems to create a mistake upon which action can change relative power in a given situation.[109]

Multidimensional coordination concerns the "coordination and cooperation among different forces in different spheres in order to accomplish an objective."[110] Purposely this includes both military and non-military entities working in concert towards a specific objective. The focus of coordination includes the military realm in addition to "'strategic resources' such as geographical factors, the role of history, cultural traditions, sense of ethnic identity, dominating

---

[107]*Sun-Tzu The Art of Warfare*, trans. and ed. Roger T. Ames, 127.

[108]Timothy L, Thomas, *The Dragon's Quantum Leap* (Fort Leavenworth, KS: Foreign Military Studies Office, 2009), 213.

[109]Qiao Liang and Wang Xiangsui, *Unrestricted Warfare*, 181-182.

[110]Ibid., 183.

and exploiting the influence of international organizations, etc."[111] Multidimensional coordination is very similar to "unified action" as described in US doctrine. *Joint Publication 3-0, Operations* describes unified action as "comprehensive approach that synchronizes, coordinates, and when appropriate, integrates military operations with the activities of other governmental and NGOs to achieve unity of effort."[112]

Omnidirectionality implies the need to dedicate cognitive efforts to gain a holistic understanding of the situation. Omnidirectionality increases the scope of what is considered in analysis and includes terrain (air, land, sea, space), "social spaces... military, politics, economics, culture, and the psyche" as battlefields with emphasis on the "technological space linking" each, referring to the technology, command, control, computers, information, and networks in use.[113] This principle applies at each level of war and across all levels of war to place PLA forces in a position from which they obtain a "field of vision with no blind spots, a concept unhindered by obstacles, and an orientation with no blind angles."[114] A corresponding concept in US Joint doctrine is the Joint Force Commander's responsibility to seek understanding within the operational environment. *Joint Publication 3-0, Operations* describes the importance of the operational environment as follows (emphasis in original):

> The JFC's **operational environment** is the composite of the conditions, circumstances, and influences that affect employment of capabilities and bear on the decisions of the commander ... It encompasses physical areas and factors (of the air, land, maritime, and space domains) and the information environment (which includes cyberspace). **Included within these are enemy, friendly, and neutral systems that are relevant to a specific**

---

[111]Ibid., 184.

[112]Joint Chiefs of Staff, *Joint Publication 3-0*, V-8.

[113]Qiao Liang and Wang Xiangsui, *Unrestricted Warfare*, 177-178.

[114]Ibid., 177.

joint operation. The nature and interaction of these systems will affect how the commander plans, organizes for, and conducts joint operations.[115]

The principle of synchrony stems from technological advancements and the resulting speed of information sharing across vast areas and audiences. From the Chinese perspective, arranging synchronous actions surpasses the need to phase operations in stages working towards the desired objective. Acknowledging the need for detailed planning, "beyond-limits war brings key factors of warfare which are dispersed in different spaces and different domains to bear in the same, designated space of time" where "[a] single full-depth, synchronized action may … be enough to decide the outcome of an entire war."[116] The emphasis remains on leveraging all resources available at and across the levels of war in "precise and well-timed offensive operations."[117] PLA synchrony appears very similar to the Western concept of parallel war. In parallel war, like synchrony, simultaneous attacks take place across the three dimensions of "time, space and levels of war – to achieve rapid dominance."[118] The object of parallel war is to "achieve effective control over the set of systems relied on by an adversary for power and influence – leadership, population, essential industry, transportation and distribution, and forces."[119] Dominance is achieved when an enemy no longer controls the very sources of its power.

---

[115]Joint Chiefs of Staff, *Joint Publication 3.0 Operations*, IV-1.

[116]Qiao Liang and Wang Xiangsui, *Unrestricted Warfare*, 178.

[117]Department of Defense, *Military and Security Developments Involving the People's Republic of China 2012*, 3.

[118]David A. Deptula, "Defining Rapid Decisive Operations: Parallel Warfare," in *Effects Based Operations: Change in the Nature of Warfare* (Arlington, Virginia: Aerospace Education Foundation, 2001), 4,5.

[119]Ibid.

The principle of minimal consumption is not simple economy, which implies a sparing or minimal use of resources. Instead, minimal consumption includes consideration of the "rational use of resources" meaning "the most appropriate method" tied to a given objective.[120] The "key to truly achieving 'minimal consumption' is to find a combat method which makes rational use of combat resources" which can include combinations of "the superiorities of several kinds of combat resources in several kinds of areas to form up a completely new form of combat, accomplishing the objective while at the same time minimizing consumption."[121] Stated another way, minimal consumption includes unique combinations that may cost more in resources in the short term, yet due to rapid success, is likely to consume less over time. US Joint doctrine describes mass in a similar way. Mass includes efforts to "concentrate the effects of combat power at the most advantageous place and time to produce decisive results… In order to achieve mass, appropriate joint force capabilities are integrated and synchronized where they will have a decisive effect in a short period of time."[122]

The last principle, adjustment and control of the entire process, includes "feedback and revisions throughout the entire course of a war."[123] In addition to the technological needs already addressed, adjustment and control relies on a commander's "intuition" to maintain situation understanding and adaptability. This principle is largely identical to the functions of assessment in US military doctrine. US *Joint Publication 3-0 Operations* describes assessment as "a process that evaluates changes in the environment and measures progress of the joint force toward mission accomplishment. Commanders continuously assess the operational environment and the

---

[120]Qiao Liang and Wang Xiangsui, *Unrestricted Warfare*, 182-183.

[121]Qiao Liang and Wang Xiangsui, *Unrestricted Warfare*, 183.

[122]Joint Chiefs of Staff, *Joint Publication 3.0, Operations*, A-2.

[123]Qiao Liang and Wang Xiangsui, *Unrestricted Warfare*, 185.

progress of operations, compare them to their initial visualization, understanding, and intent, and adjust operations based on this analysis."[124]

This section examined Chinese strategy and PLA doctrine. PLA doctrine reveals the apparently unique Chinese principles of limited objectives, unlimited measures, and asymmetry. These three principles exist without a similar United States equivalent. The remaining Chinese principles of war appear to have a similar US doctrinal principle or concept. The presence of similarities provides insight into possible universal aspects of warfare. The majority of Chinese principles of war fall in line with US DOD characterization of the PLA desire for "precise and well timed offensive operations, gaining and retaining the initiative, attacking only under favorable conditions and exploiting an opponent's most vulnerable weaknesses."[125]

Chinese national documents and PLA doctrine uncover the continuing influence of philosophical and aspects of Chinese military tradition. PLA doctrine maintains an overarching emphasis placed on asymmetric warfare, the patience and flexibility in allowing a situation to develop (*wu wei*), and creative combinations in harmony (*ho*). These principles assist a commander in arranging the right force, against a specific objective, at the right time (*shi*), in order to increase the likelihood of success. Chinese strategy and PLA doctrine reveal an emphasis on technology and information in modern warfare. The following section examines contemporary PLA operations for the reflection of the above concepts as a uniquely Chinese flavor of operational art.

---

[124]Joint Chiefs of Staff, *Joint Publication 3.0 Operations*, II-9.

[125]Department of Defense, *Military and Security Developments Involving the People's Republic of China 2012*, 3.

CASE STUDIES: OPERATIONS OF THE PEOPLE'S LIBERATIONS ARMY

This section examines PLA employment in UNPKO, anti-piracy operations, and cyber activities providing a brief background and characterization of PLA activities and seeks to identify and characterize a contemporary Chinese flavor of operational art. PLA support to UNPKO and anti-piracy operations receive attention as some interpret PLA deployments as supportive of a Chinese expansionist agenda. Cyber activities reflect one aspect of increased Chinese emphasis on information superiority. Observations of a holistic approach, the creative combination of forces (*ho*), and asymmetry, in addition to underlying philosophical concepts of *wu wei*, and *shi,* support the hypothesis that a uniquely Chinese flavor of operational art exists. The following case studies reveal a Chinese tendency for patient and purposeful decision-making, a limit on PLA integration with foreign militaries during mission execution and high levels of control over operations. Instead, PLA forces appear to favor planned engagements with host or other nations as examples of soft power, not associated with mission accomplishment.

UN Peacekeeping Operations

As of October 2012, China was the largest contributor of peacekeepers to UNPKO among the five permanent members of the United Nations Security Council, with 1,931 peacekeepers deployed in eleven United Nations peacekeeping missions.[126] PLA personnel deploy filling two functions in UNPKO - as experts on missions, commonly referred to as observers, and as peacekeeping troops, with peacekeepers being the largest category. Since occupying a seat on the United Nations Security Council in 1971, the PRC's role in peacekeeping experienced a slow start with a marked increase in 2003. The international Crisis Group presents

---

[126]United Nations Department of Peacekeeping Operations, "UN Mission's Summary detailed by Country 31 Oct 2012," under "Resources, Statistics, Troop and Police Contributors," http://www.un.org/en/peacekeeping/contributors/2012/October12_3.pdf (accessed 5 December 2012).

China's association with UNPKO as having evolved through four stages from initial opposition to participation.

The International Crisis Group authored *China's Growing Role in UN Peacekeeping*, a 2009 report in which they detail China's historic participation in UNPKO. The initial stage "opposition and non-participation" started in1971, when the PRC gained their seat in the United Nations Security Council, and lasted until 1980. China opposed interfering in another state's internal matters, viewing interference as a challenge to that state's national sovereignty. During this period, China avoided voting on UNPKO, choosing "to abstain or simply not participate in voting, thereby allowing Security Council resolutions to go forward."[127] The second stage, "limited support," lasted from 1981 to 1987 and marked China's first vote and financial contribution in support of UNPKO.[128]

The third stage lasted from 1988 to 2000, and included China's initial participation in UNPKO. During this period, China became a member of the United Nation General Assembly's Special Committee for Peacekeeping Operations and sent civilians followed by an increasing number of PLA troops, to UNPKO as observers. China's first contribution of PLA troops as peacekeepers took place between 1992 and 1993 when 800 PLA engineers deployed in support of the United Nations Transitional Authority in Cambodia. This contribution would be China's only PLA troop deployment for the next ten years.[129]

---

[127]The International Crisis Group, "China's Growing Role in UN Peacekeeping," *Asia Report* no.166 (17 April 2009), 4,5. http://www.crisisgroup.org/~/media/Files/asia/north-east-asia/166_chinas_growing_role_in_un_peacekeeping.pdf (accessed 5 December, 2012).

[128]Ibid., 5

[129]Yin He, "China's Changing Policy on UN Peacekeeping Operations," *Asia Paper* (Stockholm-Nacka, Sweden: Institute for Security and Development Policy, 2007), 24-25, http://www.isdp.eu/publications/asia-papers.html?start=50 (accessed 5 December 2012).

China's current level of support for UNPKO started with the beginning of the twenty-first century. Marked initially with the deployment of police, China began to increase both police and PLA troops contributed to UNPKO. Of note is China's increase in the number of troops contributed after 2003, which continued to climb until 2010 when it slightly declined to current levels. By the end of 2010, China claimed to have deployed a collective total of 17,390 military troops to UNPKO.[130] China's increase in support to UNPKO coincides with the decline in United States participation since 2000, as illustrated in figure 1.

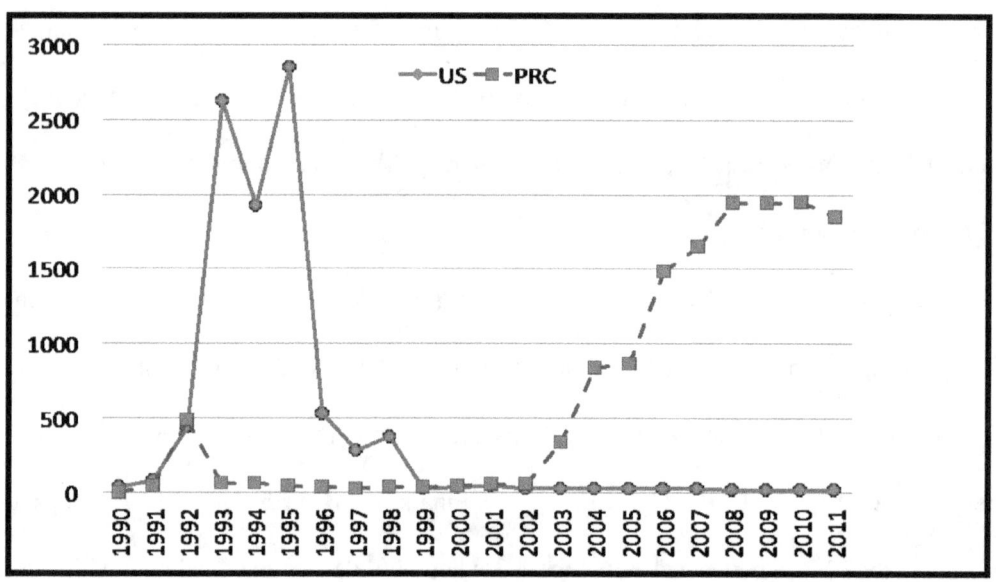

Figure 1. US and PRC Contributions to UN Peacekeeping, 1999-2011.

Source: Matthew Castillo, *"Peaceful Relations?: United Nations Peacekeeping Operations and the Military relations between the United States and the People Republic of China,"* (Master's thesis, US Army Command and General Staff College, 2012), 45.

The concept of *wu wei* as previously described provides a rationale for China's patient increase in UNPKO participation. Cautious and observant for nearly thirty years, China began to participate where there was the least opposition, first with civilian observers and then PLA

---

[130]The People's Republic of China, *China's National Defense in 2010*.

military observers, later followed by PLA peacekeepers. The practice of gradual increase changed after the year 2000. Coincident with Chinese increase was a significant reduction of US military troops in UNPKO, along with a decline in participation from other Western nations. *Wu wei* offers a possible explanation; China increased UNPKO participation in a time when doing so was least likely to generate objections or negative attention. The September 11, 2001 terrorist attacks changed immediate priorities for the United States and other Western nations. Reduced US support to UNPKO created an opportunity for the PLA to increase their participation without opposition. The venue of UNPKO effectively became a "low area" towards which the PLA could easily flow. The goal of *wu wei* is to act without friction, to be flexible and patient to the point that others propel you ahead. This aspect of *wu wei* is also reflected by China's positive response to UN requests since 2007 to increase contributions, and to play a larger role in key positions within the UN Department of Peacekeeping Operations and in UNPKO specifically.[131]

According to the International Crisis Group report, once China makes the decision to contribute peacekeepers, the Central Military Commission assigns one of the seven military regions the "responsibility for a specific deployment."[132] The tasked military region combines personnel and skill sets into a new unit for deployment. The military region then conducts pre-deployment training before PLA peacekeepers deploy on eight-month rotations in their respective peacekeeping operating areas.[133] As previously stated, PLA contributions include both observers and peacekeeping troops. Military Observers serve in small numbers throughout a UNPKO mission area and operate in multinational observer teams. PLA troop contributions are different;

---

[131]International Crisis Group, "China's Growing Role in UN Peacekeeping," 7.

[132]Ibid., 27.

[133]Bates Gill, Chin-hao Huang, "China's Expanding Role in Peacekeeping, Prospects and Policy Implications," *SIPRI Policy Paper* 25 (November 2009): 5, http://books.sipri.org/index_html?c_category_id=50 (accessed 7 December 2012).

the PLA creates formed units, *combinations* that deploy and operate as cohesive detachments. These units typically include "engineering, transportation, and medical services."[134]

The International Crisis Group report characterizes PLA peacekeepers as "[having] a very strong work ethic, are professional and very committed." [135] While PLA peacekeepers complete their tasks in a proficient manner, the report claims PLA troops "rarely take any initiative."[136] Additionally, based on the missions PLA peacekeepers conduct and the fact they deploy in self-contained formed units, their interaction with peacekeepers from other nations is limited.

PLA peacekeepers generally conduct engineering, transportation, and medical support in their given UNPKO. China's 2010 *White Paper on National Defense* claims PLA peacekeepers have "built and repaired over 8,700 km of roads and 270 bridges, cleared over 8,900 mines and various explosive devices, transported over 600,000 tons of cargo across a total distance of 9.3 million km, and treated 79,000 patients."[137] In addition to tasks covered under an assigned UN mission mandate, PLA peacekeepers establish relationships and provide support to host nation entities. These activities include cultural exchanges which display Chinese arts, support for local populations through medical care, collaboration with aid organizations, and providing donations, often of food, clothes, and computers. These efforts highlight the nationalism of PLA forces and

---

[134]Bates Gill, and Chin-hoa Huang, "China's Expanding Presence in UN Peacekeeping Operations and Implications for the United States," in *Beyond the Strait: PLA Missions Other Than Taiwan*, ed. Roy Kamphausen, David Lai and Andrew Scobell (Carlisle, PA: Strategic Studies Institute, April 2008), 106.

[135]The International Crisis Group, "China's Growing Role in UN Peacekeeping," 7.

[136]Ibid.

[137]The People's Republic of China, *China's National Defense in 2010.*

are serve to reinforce China's desire to portray itself as a great power and responsible international force for peace.[138]

The exact role of peacekeeping in the overarching PRC strategy is unknown. However, China emphasizes peacekeeping accomplishments in their *White Papers,* and continues both financial and personnel support for these missions. These facts reveal that at a minimum peacekeeping can be viewed as an example of soft power - demonstrating to the world China's desire for international peace and a responsible rise in power. According to Bates Gill and Chin-hoa Huang of the Stockholm International Peace Research Institute, multiple motivations likely support Chinese participation in UNPKO. First, based on Chinese academics with insight on Chinese leadership, peacekeeping is likely a means to "reduce tensions and conflicts in global hotspots," which benefits China's efforts to sustain and increase social and economic growth.[139]

Second, China leverages UNPKO participation to demonstrate its peaceful intent to other nations. This falls in line with China's National Defense narrative as an effort to quiet fears over increasing military capabilities. Gill and Huang classify UNPKO participation as a way to "help the PLA and police forces improve their readiness for other missions."[140] The Department of Defense's report, *Military and Security Developments Involving the People's Republic of China*

---

[138]Zhao Xiaolong and Li Minshuai, "Chinese Peacekeeping Engineers to Congo (K) Conduct Exchange Activity with Local Students," *The People's Republic of China Ministry of National Defense,* 20 December 2011, http://eng.mod.gov.cn/DefenseNews/ 2011-12/20/content_4329384.htm (accessed 8 December 2012); China Military Online, "13th Chinese Peacekeeping Medical Detachment to Congo (K) Visits SOS Children's Village," 8 February 2012, http://eng.mod.gov.cn/Peacekeeping/2012-02/08/content_4343577.htm (accessed 8 December 2012); Qing Hao and Wang Anmin, "On-the-spot report on cultural life of Chinese engineering peacekeeping force in Congo (Kinshasa)," *PLA Daily,* 26 March 2003, http://english.pladaily.com.cn/special/e-peace/txt/39.htm (accessed 22 April 2012).

[139]Bates Gill, and Chin-hoa Huang, "China's Expanding Presence in UN Peacekeeping Operations and Implications for the United States," 108.

[140]Ibid., 108-113.

2012, includes UN peacekeeping as one example of the "extent to which China's leaders are increasingly looking to the PLA to perform missions that go beyond China's immediate territorial concerns."[141]

PLA participation in UNPKO appears to support the PLA doctrinal concept of creating combinations and the contemporary influence of *wu wei*. The way PLA units are formed for peacekeeping duty is an example of a combination where the resulting unit supports UNPKO mandates. The nature of PLA accepted tasks under the UNPKO mandate typically limit interaction and integration with peacekeepers from other countries. PLA peacekeepers do interact and support host nation entities in tasks outside the respective mission mandate. These extra activities include cultural exchanges and instances of ongoing support to charities benefiting the local populace. As a reflection of *wu wei*, peacekeeping activities grew patiently as the situation developed, are unopposed and aid in shaping the perspective of PLA and China in general. In this manner, PLA peacekeeping is one element of other holistic efforts to demonstrate China as a responsible great power. A 2004 speech, delivered by former Chinese President Hu Jintao, supports this claim stating the desire for an increase in PLA activities "promoting international peace and security."[142]

This characterization of PLA employment shows a Chinese flavor of operational art where PLA actions directly support Chinese strategic goals. PLA participation in UNPKO appears to support one element of China's efforts to demonstrate positive and responsible engagement in world affairs. Additionally, the decision for PLA employment in UNPKO exhibits a slow change of perspective, and patience in waiting for a favorable situation, thus avoiding

---

[141]Department of Defense, *Military and Security Developments Involving the People's Republic of China 2012*, iv.

[142]Ibid., 3,4.

friction (*wu wei*). This analysis exposes China as patient and purposeful in expanding UNPKO participation. PLA support to UNPKO took place when and where there was little to no opposition, and was marked by an unobtrusive presence then a gradual increase over time, further reducing opposition. *Wu wei* succeeds when others actually begin to propel one ahead, a characteristic supported by post-2007 UN calls for increased Chinese participation in UNPKO.[143] China's resulting position in UNPKO and the UN Department of Peacekeeping Operations increases China's influence in UN collective bodies increasing their global presence and strategic position of power, *shi*.

Anti-Piracy operations

The PLA Navy, created in 1949, exists "independently or jointly with the Army and Air Force, to guard against enemy invasion from the sea, defend the state's sovereignty over its territorial waters, and safeguard the state's maritime rights and interests."[144] Like all branches of the PLA, the Navy has increased both the use of technology and the capability of its ships. Operationally, the PLA Navy has a history of military diplomacy where ships conduct military diplomacy through foreign port visits. PLA Navy vessels have supported diplomacy in multiple countries since the mid 1980s. China views these visits as a means to increase military engagement between PLA forces and those of the host nations.[145] In a 2004 speech, then Chinese President Hu Jintao called on the PLA Navy to extend its operational reach further from the PRC mainland to better defend Chinese interests. Accordingly, the *White Papers* issued in 2006 and

---

[143]International Crisis Group, "China's Growing Role in UN Peacekeeping," 7.

[144]The People's Republic of China, *China's National Defense in 2002* (Beijing: Information Office of the State Council of the People's Republic of China, 2002).

[145]The People's Republic of China, *China's National Defense* (Beijing: Information Office of the State Council of the People's Republic of China, July 1998).

2008 reflect an emphasis on increasing naval reach. US DOD reporting indicates continuing

debate over the degree to which this represents an understandable extension of reach while

maintaining a strategy of "Offshore Defense," or a more fundamental change to a "Far Seas

Defense" strategy.[146]

The US-China Economic and Security Review Commission links increased naval

capabilities to China's economic interests based on PLA Academy of Military Science

documents. The referenced PLA source documents claim that "Along with the continued growth

of our [Chinese] economic power and our scientific and technical level, [our] naval forces will

further expand, and our operational sea area will gradually expand out into the northern part of

the Pacific until the second island chain."[147] Highlighting economic interests, Robert Kaplan

asserts China is largely dependent, "as much as 85 percent," on oil and gas imports traveling

through the Indian Ocean and Straits of Malacca.[148] The importance of ocean-based commerce is

evident and closely tied to China's *shi* and necessitates the protection of sea lines of

communication and maritime shipping. In support of such efforts, PLA Navy participation in

anti-piracy operations began in 2008, when China deployed PLA Navy ships to the Gulf of Aden

to conduct counter-piracy operations. Prior to the first deployment in 2008, a spokesman from the

Ministry of Foreign Affairs highlighted that "China's shipping and economic interests were being

---

[146]Department of Defense, *Military and Security Developments Involving the People's Republic of China 2011* (Washington D.C.: Office of the Secretary of Defense, May 2011), 61.

[147]US-China Economic and Security Review Commission, *2012 Report to Congress*, 112th Congress, 2nd session (Washington D.C.: Government Printing Office, 2012), 144.

[148]Robert D. Kaplan, *Monsoon: The Indian Ocean and the Future of American Power* (New York, New York: Random House, 2010), 283.

threatened" and the decisions to conduct anti-piracy operations "were simply an effort to help rectify an increasingly vexing problem."[149]

China's naval deployment to the Gulf of Aden began in late 2008 with a naval task force to "escort Chinese ships sailing through the region, as well as non-Chinese ships carrying humanitarian goods, such as items for the UN World Food Program."[150] One indication of the importance placed on the first anti-piracy deployment is the selection of a high-ranking official as the commander. The chief of staff to the South Sea Fleet, Rear Admiral Du Jingcheng was selected to command the first anti-piracy deployment.[151] Chinese statements indicate that of the "1,265 Chinese commercial vessels or vessels carrying Chinese goods that traversed the region from January to November 2008, pirates attacked 20 percent of them."[152] The Chinese have maintained a presence of three ships -- one replenishment ship and two accompanying warships since the initial deployment. The warships have included a mix of frigates and or destroyers, their associated crew, plus "70 special operations forces."[153]

Now in its thirteenth rotation, which began in November 2012, the PLA Navy has increased coordination with members of the Combined Task Force-151, comprised of United States, European, and other contributing countries conducting counter-piracy under a United

---

[149]Christopher D. Yung, Ross Rustici, Isaac Kardon, and Joshua Wiseman, *China Strategic Perspectives, China's Out of Area Naval Operations: Case Studies, Trajectories, Obstacles, and Potential Solutions* (Washington D.C.: National Defense University, Institute for National Strategic Studies, 2010.), 5.

[150]US-China Economic and Security Review Commission, *2009 Report to Congress*, 111th Congress, 1st session, 119.

[151]Yung, et al., *China Strategic Perspectives*, 5.

[152]Ibid.

[153]Ibid., 119, 135-136.

Nations Security Council resolution.[154] PLA Navy coordination with Combined Task Force-151 has included direct coordination with Japanese and Indian naval components. Additionally, in 2012, the first United States and Chinese Navy "joint anti-piracy drill" took place.[155] The exercise included the "USS *Winston S. Churchill* and the Chinese frigate *Yi Yang*" in a "joint visit, board, search, and seizure scenario."[156] Chinese media reported the event as "conducive to increasing mutual understanding and trust between the two navies and deepening bilateral cooperation in non-conventional security fields."[157]

While coordination has increased with other anti-piracy efforts in the region, the PLA Navy presence remains independent from North Atlantic Treaty Organization efforts and Combined Task Force-151 also operating under the UN Security Council resolution. The coordination includes mainly deconfliction but not necessarily integration. US Congressional testimony describes the Chinese activity: "The PLA Navy maintains its own escort corridor off the coast of Somalia in the Gulf of Aden and does not participate in multination antipiracy task forces. While cooperation between China and European actors is minimal, it acts to reinforce mutually shared imperatives and norms regarding maritime security."[158] Chinese ships patrol their own area of operations and limit their support to ships from China, Taiwan, and ships supporting

---

[154]US-China Economic and Security Review Commission, *2009 Report to Congress*, 119. Zhu Shaobin and Xiao Jiancheng, "13th Chinese naval escort taskforce arrives in Gulf of Aden," *Peopl'e Daily Online*, (2012). http://english.peopledaily.com.cn/90786/8031368.html (accessed 12 December 2012).

[155]US-China Economic and Security Review Commission, *2012 Report to Congress*, 112th Congress, 2nd session, 135-136.

[156]Ibid., 143.

[157]"China, US conduct first joint anti-piracy drill," *English Xinhua*, September 18, 2012, http://news.xinhuanet.com/english/china/2012-09/18/c_131856143.htm (accessed Oct 1, 2012).

[158]US-China Economic and Security Review Commission, *2012 Report to Congress*, 318.

international organizations carrying humanitarian aid.[159] Chinese naval operations over the last three years in the Gulf of Aden reveal the weight placed on securing Chinese economic interests.[160]

The stated Chinese strategic objectives - to sustain economic growth and development, maintain internal stability, and defend national sovereignty and territorial integrity - require naval power to protect sea lines of communication. Kaplan highlights China's acquisition of energy from global markets as necessitating a blue-water navy to secure sea transportation. As China increases its demand for energy resources, the ability to ensure the arrival of goods becomes more important to their national interests. Kaplan asserts that China is likely to further increase its naval presence along major shipping routes and seek "access to modern deepwater ports in friendly countries."[161] DOD reporting supports a Chinese desire for either "traditional military 'bases,' suited for supporting distant combat operations, or a more limited set of logistical supply 'places,' that are better suited to peacetime deployments, such as counter-piracy and HA/DR [humanitarian assistance/disaster response]."[162] From this perspective, "China's demand for energy motivates both its foreign policy and national security policy: the need for an increasing, uninterrupted flow of energy to sustain its dramatic economic growth," requiring the PLA Navy to continue counter piracy escorts in vital shipping lanes.[163]

---

[159]"China Navy's Escorting Missions in Gulf of Aden, Somali Waters," *People's Daily Online*, (2009) http://english.people.com.cn/90002/96181/index.html (accessed 10 December 2012). US-China Economic and Security Review Commission, "2012 Report to Congress," 318.

[160]US-China Economic and Security Review Commission, *2012 Report to Congress*, 134.

[161]Kaplan, *Monsoon,* 11.

[162]Department of Defense, *Military and Security Developments Involving the People's Republic of China 2011*, 61.

[163]Kaplan, *Monsoon*, 282.

The PLA Navy, like the PLA in peacekeeping, is operating in support of strategic objectives. In this case, PLA Navy operations assist in securing Chinese economic growth and development through protecting sea commerce. Additionally, PLA Navy ships that support anti-piracy operations often conduct port calls increasing military diplomacy. In 2012, PLA ships completing the eleventh anti-piracy rotation entered the Black Sea for the first time, then made multiple port calls before visiting Israel, another first in port call locations.[164] The use of a navy in military diplomacy is not unique to China. PLA Navy activities when deployed reveal efforts to display China's power in the ability to project sea power and to do so in a responsible manner reflecting China's harmonious image.

General characterizations of PLA Navy activities reveal a clear tie to Chinese strategic goals and limited interaction with other national navies in the execution of anti-piracy operations. *China Strategic Perspectives*, a publication from the Institute for National Strategic Studies, characterizes PLA Navy operations. "Examination of the history of China's out of area operations indicates that the Chinese have been operating out of area since the mid-1970s, they tend to "overprepare" for each out of area deployment, and they conduct deployments not only for operational reasons, but also for carefully calculated political benefits."[165] The calculated nature is further revealed in the high level of selected commanders to command and control these operations. The tendency to "overprepare" likely exists for multiple reasons that range from practical wisdom to concerns over failure. There is a correlation between this tendency and the PLA doctrine principle of unlimited measures, which empower a commander to seek all possible resources available then apply them without "restrictions, beyond boundaries, to accomplish

---

[164]US-China Economic and Security Review Commission, *2012 Report to Congress*, 136. Port calls included Bulgaria, Romania, Ukraine, and Israel.

[165]Yung, et al., *China Strategic Perspectives*, 1.

limited objectives."[166] While not clearly linked to principles introduced as philosophical or relating to China's military tradition, PLA Navy anti-piracy operations show a high degree of control in the preparation and execution of PLA Navy operations.

The 2004 *White Paper* provides a good context for viewing PLA Navy operations. The *White Paper* addresses military exchanges, and exercises as a means to "enhance the joint capabilities" of the PLA and learn from "foreign armed forces…to advance the modernization of the Chinese armed forces."[167] In addition to military benefits stated, military-to-military engagements are another element of Chinese soft power to influence international perceptions.

PLA Navy operations continue to reflect patience and purposeful increases (*wu wei*) allowing the situation to develop. Anti-piracy operations are characterized as taking place under a high degree of control and calculated preparation as they support China's economic interests. A commonality with UNPKO support is the PLA Navy limitations on integration with other national forces. Interaction with other national navies or populations is limited to prearranged exercises or in instances of military diplomacy through port calls. Since PLA navy anti-piracy operations are only now entering their fourth year, it is likely they are continuing to learn about the environment. As China continues its naval presence in the Gulf of Aden, *wu wei* implies the PLA Navy will adjust their position within the environment to save energy and reduce risks or opposition. The limitations placed on integrating with foreign navies may indicate an attempt at risk reductions.

---

[166]Qiao Liang and Wang Xiangsui, *Unrestricted Warfare*, 181.

[167]The People's Republic of China, *China's National Defense in 2004.*

Cyber warfare activities

China's official public emphasis on cyber activities includes both Chinese national and PLA doctrine presented above which stresses "informationalizing" the PLA. This effort includes a holistic upgrade of PLA equipment and systems to "win local wars under the conditions of informationalization" and includes weapon systems, automation of command and control systems, and an increase in information technology expertise and application.[168] As a component of informationalization, cyber activity emerged in China prior to 1999. During its infancy, there was no direct attribution to the Chinese government.

Timothy Thomas, a subject matter expert on Chinese cyber activities, details two Chinese "cyber wars" that took place in 1999, the first against the United States and the second against Taiwan. After a US bomb stuck the Chinese Embassy in Belgrade, Yugoslavia on 8 May, US and Chinese entities engaged in a "network battle." The cyber activity included defacing websites and overloading network servers thus blocking access to some US government and civilian websites. Thomas reports, "Chinese hackers broke into nearly 1,000 US civilian websites and coordinated an attack on NATO computers."[169] In August of the same year, a "cyber war" took place between Chinese and Taiwanese hackers after the Taiwanese president made statements challenging China's claim of sovereignty over Taiwan. Hackers on each side targeted government-associated websites in harassment style operations. Assessments after both instances indicate the "hackers"

---

[168]The People's Republic of China, *China's National Defense in 2004* (Beijing: Information Office of the State Council of the People's Republic of China, 2004).

[169]Timothy L. Thomas, *The Internet in China: Civilian and Military Uses*, Foreign Military Studies Office, Fort Leavenworth, KS (2001) http://fmso.leavenworth.army.mil/ documents/china-internet.htm (accessed 9 December 2012).

operated within China; however, investigations revealed no official links to the Chinese government.[170]

As Joseph Nye highlights in *Cyber Power*, "[p]roof of the origin or motive of such attacks is often very difficult as attackers can route their intrusions through servers in other countries to make attribution difficult."[171] The writers of *Unrestricted Warfare*, both PLA colonels, appear to leverage this difficulty by asserting that those who conduct cyber activities are not limited to government or PLA personnel, instead cyber activity also includes the use of "hackers" to "impair the security of an army or a nation in a major way."[172]

In 2009, US rhetoric changed from vague assertions of cyber activity emerging from China to a clear accusation. The 2009 US-China Economic and Security Review Commission's report to Congress asserts that China relies on "cyber espionage" where "Chinese hackers use pilfered information to advance political, economic, and security objectives."[173] The report lists targets of Chinese cyber activities as "intellectual property and trade secrets" within private industries. Additionally, the "US defense industrial base and a range of government and military targets" have been targeted by Chinese cyber activities.[174] The nature of these targets and investigations using forensic analysis, point towards Chinese state sponsorship of cyber activity.[175] The 2009 US-China Economic and Security Review Commission "implicates the

---

[170]Ibid.

[171]Joseph S. Nye Jr., *Cyber Power* (Cambridge, MA: Harvard Kennedy School, 2010), 6.

[172]Qiao Liang and Wang Xiangsui, *Unrestricted Warfare*, 33.

[173]US-China Economic and Security Review Commission, *2012 Report to Congress*, 147.

[174]Ibid.

[175]US-China Economic and Security Review Commission, *2009 Report to Congress*,169.

Chinese government directly, or sometimes even specific parts of the Chinese government, such as the People's Liberation Army" in cyber activities targeting the United States.[176]

The report further asserts the PLA established civilian units to integrate military and non-military technical expertise in dedicated, and growing, cyber units as early as 1998. Recruiting efforts targeted "politically reliable" civilians with technical and foreign language skills to increase intelligence collection through cyber means. Emphasis on technical skills was evident in relaxed PLA standards meant to draw the right skill sets and people.[177] *Unrestricted Warfare* describes PLA troop reductions in the nineteen eighties to change from quantity and physical strength to quality and mental abilities. In the resulting perspective a "pasty-faced scholar wearing thick eyeglasses is better suited to be a modern soldier."[178] These cyber-savvy individuals emerged within China as a new type of fighter in the realm of information warfare. Qiao and Wang note the difficulty in tracing the origins and characterizing intent and affiliation of the individuals conducting cyber activities as a clear strength. The actual individuals, regardless of association, can hide among a realm of possible actors, be they individuals motivated by a multitude of reasons or a state sponsored professional cadre of cyber operators.[179]

The 2012 US-China Economic and Security Review Commission's report to Congress provides additional information on Chinese-sanctioned cyber activities that includes PLA involvement. Specifically, the following reflects current estimates of PLA units and their associated cyber focus:

---

[176]Ibid.

[177]Ibid., 173.

[178]Qiao Liang and Wang Xiangsui, *Unrestricted Warfare*, 32.

[179]Ibid., 33-34.

Second Department, PLA General Staff Department: conducts military intelligence activities, possible use of cyber in collection efforts.

Third Department, PLA General Staff Department: conducts signals intelligence, computer network exploitation efforts, and "may also lead PLA's computer network defense efforts."

Fourth Department, PLA General Staff Department: conducts electronic warfare activities, indications link the Fourth Department with computer network attack.

PLA services operate "Technical Reconnaissance Bureaus" believed to conduct computer network operations.

Cyber warfare militias: "A subset of the PLA militia has cyber-related responsibilities. These units, usually comprised of workers with high-tech day jobs, focus on various aspects of military communications, electronic warfare, and computer network operations."[180]

Characterizing the intent of PLA units, the 2009 US-China Economic and Security Review Commission referenced a Chinese municipal government job advertisement. A local information warfare militia unit sought individuals willing to work peacetime and wartime activities described as "research and exercises related to network warfare, and continuously improving methods for network attacks. ...In peacetime, extensively collect information from adversary networks and establish databases of adversary network data. ...In wartime, attack adversary network systems, and resist enemy network attacks."[181] Linking this advertisement with the apparent targets of Chinese cyber activities is worth noting. By targeting private industry's intellectual property and trade secrets in addition to government, military, and the US industrial base in time of peace, China gathers intelligence important in support of both Chinese strategic objectives and any future asymmetric applications in cyber attack or defense operations.

---

[180]US-China Economic and Security Review Commission, *2012 Report to Congress*, 149-150.

[181]US-China Economic and Security Review Commission, *2009 Report to Congress*, 174.

The DOD asserts that China's use of cyber intrusions "indicates the likelihood that Beijing is using cyber network operations (CNOs) as a tool to collect strategic intelligence.[182] Under this umbrella, elements of the PLA and likely other governmental entities "play a central role in implementing Chinese policy in cyberspace."[183] The importance of cyber activities is further reflected in *The Science of Military Strategy*, as serving strategic functions and a "primary task of the modern warfare" in order to negate or neutralize technologically linked systems, weapons and persons operating in concert, gaining an asymmetric advantage.[184] In this manner, cyber attacks are likely as an element of future combinations with conventional forces aimed at negating or creating a weakness in their enemy (a stratagem) to exploit with PLA strengths (asymmetry).

The nature of cyber activity fits well within the use of *wu wei*, stratagems and *shi*. *Wu Wei* includes taking action where little to no opposition exists. The anonymity of cyber activities supports the practice of *wu wei* in the ability to act without opposition. Additionally, even though "the agent may be scarcely noticed, his or her influence is in fact decisive."[185] Stratagems are used to cause an enemy to make mistakes and rest on a detailed knowledge of an enemy to be successful. The current targets of Chinese cyber activities are likely the result of intelligence collection for future use in stratagems. Finally, cyber activities make up a modern realm of virtual *shi*. Chinese use of cyber activities to gain knowledge on possible adversaries supports their

---

[182]Department of Defense, *Military and Security Developments Involving the People's Republic of China 2012*, 9.

[183]US-China Economic and Security Review Commission, *2012 Report to Congress*, 148.

[184]Peng Quangqian and Yao Youzhi, *The Science of Military Strategy*, 339.

[185]Ibid., Kindle Locations 4400-4401.

ability to gain a position of advantage, either to identify enemy weaknesses or leverage capabilities to negate enemy strengths.

Leveraging cyber activities for intelligence purposes and espionage better enables PLA asymmetric warfare efforts – a uniquely Chinese underpinning of operational art. Specifically, cyber activities provide an asymmetric contribution as a component of future combinations, seeking to increase advantages and negate enemy strengths. Drawing on Chinese perceptions of US military reliance on information and computer networking in the Gulf War, *combinations (ho)* will include cyber activities in the future. In this manner, cyber activities attempt to "disrupt [enemy] information acquisition and information transfer, launching a virus attack or hacking to sabotage information processing and information utilization."[186]

While the pursuit of technology and cyber capabilities is not unique to China, the motivation behind China's specific efforts appear to be linked to their philosophical foundation (*wu wei*) and military tradition (stratagems, asymmetry, and *shi*). As described, cyber activities are expected to play a role in contemporary PLA operations under the principles of asymmetry, unlimited measures, and synchrony. This study suggests Chinese use of cyber will continue where least likely to generate opposition and focus on the collection of strategic intelligence to be applied in stratagems and in seeking an asymmetric advantage in a conflict.

A Chinese Flavor of Operational Art Reflected in Case Studies

Common to all case studies is a clear link to Chinese strategic goals. Each activity of the PLA can be traced to supporting China's stated strategic goals of "preserving Communist Party rule, sustaining economic growth and development, defending national sovereignty and territorial integrity, achieving national unification, maintaining internal stability, and securing China's

---

[186]US-China Economic and Security Review Commission, *2009 Report to Congress*, 171-172.

status as a great power."[187] Additionally, case studies reveal a holistic and purposeful approach to these objectives.

UNPKO and anti-piracy operations reveal a patient increase in the activities of PLA and limited interaction with other military forces. UNPKO participation grew over a period of thirty years to its current form, with its rapid increase only taking place since 2003. PLA Navy anti-piracy operations took approximately four years to being after President Hu's speech calling for greater naval projection. A counter argument asserts PLA operations in UNPKO or in anti-piracy operations took place after equipment or technological capabilities were gained. Instead, the nature of these operations does not appear to require advanced equipment. According to the UN Department of Peacekeeping Operations, the "most common sort of UN peacekeeper is the infantry soldier."[188] Similarly, the PLA Navy has been involved in military diplomacy through port calls since 1985. Additionally, both the units formed prior to a given UNPKO deployment and PLA Navy ships sent to anti-piracy operations are limited in their integration with other nations during mission execution. The philosophical and military traditions of China examined in this study do not explain or provide insight into the purpose of such limitations.

PLA cyber activity presents the clearest examples of the fruits of China's investment in information and technology. As conveyed above, cyber capabilities enable the PLA and China as a whole to gather intelligence on military and civilian targets in support of China's continued security and economic growth. Chinese cyber targeting of US trade secrets, private industry, military industrial base, and government entities indicates efforts beyond military application in support of China's strategic goals. Additionally, the cyber environment allows Chinese operators

---

[187]Department of Defense, *Military and Security Developments Involving the People's Republic of China 2012*, 2.

[188]United Nations Department of Peacekeeping Operations, *United Nations Peacekeeping Issues*, http://www.un.org/en/peacekeeping/issues/military.shtml (accessed 16 February 2013).

a level of anonymity from which to conduct intelligence gathering without opposition for future asymmetric applications.

The case studies on PLA non-combat activities show a deliberate and sometimes slow advance in operations to allow time for the situation to develop. Additionally, the case studies expose the presence of purposeful control over interaction with forces from other nations and a willingness to interact with host nation population to exercise soft power as a positive influence of China in the international community. Throughout each case study, the philosophical concepts of *wu wei*, the pursuit of action without opposition that results in momentum, and *shi* as the pursuit of a position of strategic advantage, are evident. The PLA is one indirect aspect of a Chinese holistic approach to *shi*, meant to increase its strategic power potential in the world, and in the case of cyber activities, to increase an asymmetric advantage over possible adversaries.

CONCLUSION

This study examined China's predominant philosophical and military tradition, contemporary doctrine, and modern operations to answer the primary research question: *Does contemporary PLA doctrine and activity indicate a uniquely Chinese way of thinking and practice in operational art, influenced by philosophy and military tradition?* Analysis suggests that a Chinese flavor of operational art does in fact exist, and that it is different from that of US operational art.

This study asserts the importance of history, specifically relating to China's unique philosophical and military tradition, as a lens through which to increase understanding of modern PLA operational art. The philosophical ideas present in Confucianism and Taoism bring clarity to efforts to characterize contemporary PLA activities. First, the concept of *yin and yang* establishes a worldview within which military power can alter a situation into its polar opposite, where the weak can act in a given situation to become strong.[189] Second, the pursuit of harmony (*ho*), underpins actions to creatively "make the most of any situation," striving for the "quality of the combination at any one moment created by effectively correlating and contextualizing" all available means.[190] Next, the concept of *wu wei* stresses holistic understanding and patience. The practitioner of *wu wei* seeks holistic understanding of a situation and environment in order to remain flexible, to act without opposition to gain a desired position relative an adversary. These three philosophical concepts are foundational to China's military tradition.

Sun Tzu's concept of *shi* and the pursuit of asymmetry illustrate China's military tradition. *Shi* concerns the potential power within a given situation. *Shi* is both a position from which to release power, and an end state from which one maintains such an advantage and is able to "subdue the enemy without fighting."[191] The second topic stressed by Sun Tzu is asymmetry, where one seeks to apply strengths against an enemy's specific weaknesses. Asymmetry continues to be a desired *way* to employ military force within the PLA.

The study next examined Chinese government and military documents and uncovers three broad areas of emphasis that build on China's philosophical and military tradition. First, China views the pursuit of national goals *holistically*, where all elements of power are leveraged in "preserving Communist Party rule, sustaining economic growth and development, defending national sovereignty and territorial integrity, achieving national unification, maintaining internal stability, and securing China's status as a great power."[192] Second, building on the creative nature

---

[189]*Sun-Tzu The Art of Warfare*, trans. and ed. Roger T. Ames, 52, 78.

[190]Ibid., 59, 62.

[191]Ibid., 111.

[192]Department of Defense, *Military and Security Developments Involving the People's Republic of China 2012*, 2.

of harmony, PLA doctrine stresses task-organization of all available government capabilities into *combinations*. These *combinations* extend the boundary of war into all spheres of government action, using all the country's resources together to achieve China's national goals. *Information* is the third area emphasized. Information includes the adoption of advanced technologies and information superiority, supported by current cyber activities.

The comparison of PLA doctrine with US doctrinal concepts exposed numerous similarities. Where differences exist, the principles of limited objectives, unlimited means, and asymmetry characterize a unique flavor of Chinese operational art. Together, limited objectives and unlimited means seek to conduct "well timed offensive operations" only when "favorable conditions" exist while "exploiting an opponent's most vulnerable weaknesses" (asymmetry).[193]

Finally, the PLA demonstrates two characteristics in the case studies examined that point to a unique Chinese flavor of operational art. First, PLA operations appear to progress slowly and cautiously. Instead of viewing this slow Chinese progress as a negative– an inability to reach goals quickly – it is likely that the concepts of *wu wei*, the use of stratagems, and asymmetry are at play, making this slow progress desirable in the Chinese view. The second characteristic of PLA operations is a high degree of control over PLA activities and limited integration with forces from other nations.

A unique Chinese flavor of operational art exists and reveals the continuing influence of China's philosophical and military tradition. Chinese operational art includes the creative combination of unconventional means (*ho*), the ability to alter relative positions between opposites (*yin* and *yang*), and the flexible application of forces within a situation (*wu wei*). When these elements are used collectively, they result in combinations and operations employed

---

[193]Department of Defense, *Military and Security Developments Involving the People's Republic of China 2012*, 3.

asymmetrically to create a position of relative advantage (*shi*). Contemporary and future PLA operations are likely to include a preference for an indirect approach and reveal patience in decision-making and tempo, allowing a situation to develop into a favorable condition as leaders pursue a holistic understanding of the situation, self, and enemy. Chinese operational art is distinct from US operational art and can be characterized by their unique philosophical and military tradition.

BIBLIOGRAPHY

Bower, Ernest Z. *China Reveals Its Hand on ASEAN in Phnom Penh.* July 20, 2012. http://csis.org/publication/china-reveals-its-hand-asean-phnom-penh (accessed November 17, 2012).

Chairman, Joint Chiefs of Staff. *Joint Publication 5-0, Joint Operations Planning.* Washington D.C.: Government Printing Office, 2011.

China Military Online. "13th Chinese Peacekeeping Medical Detachment to Congo (K) Visits SOS Children's Village." *China Military Online,* 8 February 2012. http://eng.mod.gov. cn/Peacekeeping/2012-02/08/content_4343577.htm (accessed 5 December April 2012).

Cordesman, Anthony H., and Nicholas S. Yarosh. *Chinese Military Modernization and Force Development, A Western Perspective.* Center for Strategic and International Studies, 2012.

Department of Defense. *Annual Report to Congress on Military and Security Developments Involving the People's Republic of China 2010.* Washington D.C.: Government Printing Office, 2010.

—. *Annual Report to Congress on Military and Security Developments Involving the People's Republic of China 2012.* Washington D.C., 2012.

—. *Sustaining US Global Leadership: Priorities for 21st Century Defense.* Washington D.C., 2012.

Deptula, David A. "Defining Rapid Decisive Operations: Parallel Warfare." In *Effects Based Operations: Change in the Nature of Warfare,* Arlington, Virginia: Aerospace Education Foundation, 2001: 4-6.

Epstein, Robert M. *Napoleon's Last Victory.* Lawrence, Kansas: University Press of Kansas, 1994.

Gill, Bates, and Chin-hoa Huang. "China's Expanding Presence in UN Peacekeeping Operations and Implications for the United States." In *Beyond the Strait: PLA Missions Other Than Taiwan,* edited by Roy Kamphausen, David Lai, and Andrew Scobell, 99-125. Carlisle, PA: Strategic Studies Institute, April 2008.

—. "China's Expanding Role in Peacekeeping, Prospects and Policy Implications." *SIPRI Policy Paper* 25, 2009. http://books.sipri.org/index_html?c_category_id=50 (accessed 5 December 2012).

Guangqian, Peng, and Yao Youzhi . *The Science of Military Strategy.* Beijing: Military Science Publishing House, Academy of Military Science, Chinese People's Liberation Army, 2005.

He, Yin. "China's Changing Policy on UN Peacekeeping Operations." *Asia Paper* Stockholm-Nacka, Sweden: Institute for Security and Development Policy, 2007. http://www.isdp. eu/publications/asia-papers.html?start=50 (accessed 5 December 2012).

Headquarters, Department of the Army. *Army Doctrine Reference Publication (ADRP) 3-0.* Washington D.C.: Government Printing Office, 2012.

Hao, Qing and Wang Anmin. "On-the-spot report on cultural life of Chinese engineering peacekeeping force in Congo (Kinshasa)." *PLA Daily*, 26 March 2003. http://english.pladaily.com.cn/special/e-peace/txt/39.htm (accessed 5 December 2012).

Jullien, Francois. *A Treatise on Efficacy.* Translated by Janet Lloyd. Honolulu: University of Hawaii Press, 2004.

Kaplan, Robert D. *Monsoon: The Indian Ocean and the Future of American Power.* New York: Random House, 2010.

Lai, David. *Learning from the Stones: A GO Approach to Mastering Chine's Strategic Concept, Shi.* Monograph, Strategic Studies Institute, Carlisle: Strategic Studies Institute, 2004.

Liang, Qiao, and Wang Xiangsui. *Unrestricted Warfare, China's Master Plan to Destroy America.* Panama City, Panama: Pan American Publishing Company, 2002.

Mott IV, William H., and Jae Chang Kim. *The Philosophy of Chinese Military Culture.* New York: Palgrave MacMillian, 2006.

Nye, Joseph S. *Cyber Power.* Cambridge: Center for Science and International Affairs, Harvard Kennedy School, 2010.

People's Daily Online. "China Navy's Escorting Missions in Gulf of Aden, Somali Waters," *People's Daily Online*, (2009) http://english.people.com.cn/90002/96181/index.html (accessed 10 December 2012).

Porter, Patrick. *Military Orientalism.* New York: Columbia University Press, 2009.

Schneider, James J. *Vulcan's Anvil.* Ft Leavenworth: School of Advanced Military Studies/US Army Command and General Staff College, 1992.

Scobell, Andrew. *China and Strategic Culture.* Strategic Studies Institute, Carlisle: Carlisle Barracks, 2002.

—. *China's Use of Military Force, Beyond the Great Wall and the Long March.* New York: Cambridge University Press, 2003.

—. "The Chinese Way of War." In *The Evolution of Operational Art from Napoleon to the Present*, edited by John Andreas Olsen and Martin Van Creveld, 195-221. New York: Oxford University Press Inc., 2011.

Sun-Tzu. *Sun-Tzu The Art of Warfare.* Edited and translated by Roger T. Ames. New York: Ballantine Books, 1993.

—. *Sun Tzu: The Art of War.* Edited and translated by Samuel B. Griffith. New York: Oxford University Press, 1971.

—. *Sun Tzu Art of War.* Edited and translated by Ralph D. Sawyer. Colorado: Westview Press Inc.,1994.

The International Crisis Group. "China's Growing Role in UN Peacekeeping." *Asia Report* no.166 (17 April 2009). http://www.crisisgroup.org/~/media/Files/asia/north-eastasia/166_chinas_growing_role_in_un_peacekeeping.pdf (accessed 5 2012).

The People's Republic of China. *China's National Defense.* Beijing: Information Office of the State Council, People's Republic of China, 1998.

—. *China's National Defense in 2000.* Beijing: Information Office of the State Council, People's Republic of China, 2000.

—. *China's National Defense in 2002.* Beijing: Information Office of the State Council, People's Republic of China, 2002.

—. *China's National Defense in 2004.* Beijing: Information Office of the State Council, People's Republic of China, 2004.

—. *China's National Defense in 2006.* Beijing: Information Office of the State Council, People's Republic of China, 2006.

—. *China's National Defense in 2008.* Beijing: Information Office of the State Council, People's Republic of China, 2009.

—. *China's National Defense in 2010.* Beijing: Information Office of the State Council, People's Republic of China, 2011.

Thomas, Timothy L. "The Chinese Military's Strategic Mind-set." *Military Review* (Headquarters, Department of the Army, US Army Combined Arms Center), November 2007: 47-55.

—. *The Internet in China: Civilian and Military Uses.* Foreign Military Studies Office, Fort Leavenworth, KS (2001) http://fmso.leavenworth.army.mil/documents/china-internet.htm (accessed 9 December 2012).

United Nations Department of Peacekeeping Operations. "United Nations Peacekeeping Issues." http://www.un.org/en/peacekeeping/issues/military.shtml (accessed 16 February 2013).

United States-China Economic and Security Review Commission. *2009 Report to Congress,* 112th Congress, 2nd session. Washington D.C.: Government Printing Office, 2012.

United States-China Economic and Security Review Commission. *2012 Report to Congress,* 112th Congress, 2nd session. Washington D.C.: Government Printing Office, 2012.

Xiaolong, Zhao and Li Minshuai. "Chinese Peacekeeping Engineers to Congo (K) Conduct Exchange Activity with Local Students." *The People's Republic of China Ministry of National Defense,* 20 December 2011. http://eng.mod.gov.cn/DefenseNews/2011-12/20/content_4329384.htm (accessed 5 December 2012).

Xinhua. "China, US conduct first joint anti-piracy drill." *English Xinhua*, September 18, 2012, http://news.xinhuanet.com/english/china/2012-09/18/c_131856143.htm (accessed Oct 1, 2012).

Yung, Christopher D., Ross Rustici, Isaac Kardon, and Joshua Wiseman. *China Strategic Perspectives, China's Out of Area Naval Operations: Case Studies, Trajectories, Obstacles, and Potential Solutions.* Washington D.C.: National Defense University, Institute for National Strategic Studies, 2010.

Zhu Shaobin and Xiao Jiancheng. *13th Chinese Naval Escort Taskforce Arrives in Gulf of Aden.* November 23, 2012. http://english.peopledaily.com.cn/90786/8031368.html (accessed December 12, 2012)